STATUES
ON THE HILL

THE STORY OF
BAUGHMAN MEMORIAL PARK

Statues
on the Hill

The Story of
Baughman Memorial Park

Aaron J. Keirns

Howard, Ohio

To my family.

Other books by Aaron J. Keirns

Black Hand Gorge...A Journey Through Time
The illustrated history of a spectacular river gorge in Licking County, Ohio.
Includes chapters on the Ohio & Erie Canal, railroad, electric interurban railway and more.
Contains over 150 photographs & illustrations.
Soft cover, 130 pages.

Ohio's Airship Disaster (2nd edition)
The illustrated story of the tragic crash of America's first rigid dirigible, the USS Shenandoah. On a September morning in 1925, the giant airship was ripped apart by a storm and fell to earth in pieces in rural Noble County, Ohio. The ship's captain and 13 of his men died in the crash. Thousands of curiosity-seekers swarmed to the crash sites, stripping the carcass of the great ship almost bare. Army troops had to be called in to maintain control.
This Second Edition contains over 100 photographs & illustrations.
Soft cover, 76 pages.

To order:
All books by this author can be ordered directly from the publisher.

For more information, visit our web site at:

www.littleriverpublishing.com

Statues on the Hill
ISBN 0-9647800-4-6

Statues on the Hill. Copyright © 2001-2008 Little River Publishing. Printed and bound in the United States of America. All rights reserved. No part of this book may be used or reproduced in any manner whatsoever – except by a reviewer who may quote brief passages in a review – without written permission from the publisher. Please address inquiries to Little River Publishing, 23700 Cornish Rd., Howard, Ohio 43028.

Although the author and publisher have made every effort to ensure the accuracy and completeness of the information contained in this book, we assume no responsibility for errors, inaccuracies, omissions, or any inconsistency herein. Any slights of people, places or organizations are unintentional. The information printed herein was obtained from a variety of sources including old books, newspapers, photographs, documents and personal interviews. Due to the historical nature of the subject matter, accuracy is not always certain. Due to the age of many of the photographs, the photographer or copyright-holder often could not be determined. The publisher welcomes comments from readers. Book design by the author.

Howard, Ohio

CONTENTS

Preface 6

The Sculptor 8

A Dedication From the Past 9

Introduction
Statues on the Hill 11

Chapter One
A Hill of Stone 14

Chapter Two
A Boy Inspired 17

Chapter Three
Statues Rise from the Quarry 28

Chapter Four
The Statues 33-71

    William McKinley 33
    Abraham Lincoln 37
    James B. McPherson 41
    James Garfield 45
    Ulysses S. Grant 49
    George Washington 53
    The Doughboy 57
    William T. Sherman 61
    Theodore Roosevelt 65
    Warren G. Harding 69

Chapter Five
Odds & Ends Around the Park 73

Map of Baughman Park 76-77
About the Author 78
Acknowledgements 78-79
Glossary of Terms 80
Bibliography 81

Left: Brice Baughman chisels the final details into General McPherson, ca. 1914.

Front Cover: The sculptor (top row with arms crossed) poses with soldiers and dignitaries during the dedication of his Doughboy statue in 1921.

Preface

I first heard about Baughman Park several years ago while doing research for a book on nearby Black Hand Gorge. While reading about the old electric interurban railway that ran between Columbus, Newark and Zanesville, I came across a brief mention of a "weird attraction" called "Baufman Park" that once existed a short distance northeast of Black Hand Gorge. The short paragraph said that an undertaker had carved stone statues of political and historical leaders on a large hill and that he "…applied quaint designs to all stones and rocks he could find."

I asked several local people about the park and some remembered going there as children in the 1920's and 30's to picnic. I was told that the property had changed hands several times over the years and that the statues were probably long gone by now. Even so, I thought there might be some remnants of the carvings still there and I decided to take a look.

My first visit to the park was by motorcycle. I turned north from State Route 16 onto State Route 586 and began climbing the steep hill. Surprisingly, when I crested the hill there was a faded wooden sign that read *Baughman Park*. I turned into the gravel drive and slowly rolled along through the sun-dappled woods, looking on either side for any evidence of carvings. I saw nothing. It was late summer and the woods were thick with foliage and brush. I soon realized that remnants of statues would be difficult to find in this overgrown area. Suddenly I saw something that made me stop and turn off my engine. There, right in front of me, was a statue of Warren G. Harding standing 12 feet tall!

It was a magic moment. I was amazed by what I saw. I climbed off the motorcycle and walked around the statue in disbelief. Even more incredible was what I found when I went further down the road. A larger-than-life statue of Teddy Roosevelt standing high on a rock ledge. Smaller figures peering out at me from the weeds along the road: a ghostly horse head emerging from a rock; a crucifix; an Indian with raised tomahawk, and a variety of odd faces. Then I came upon statues of William McKinley and Abe Lincoln standing proudly in the front yard of a dilapidated house. It was a strange scene, eerie and surreal.

I knocked on the door of a residence near the road and found the owner of the property. He charged me a dollar for the privilege of exploring the hill. I grabbed my camera from my saddlebag and started walking. Every new statue and carving I found was a new thrill. First a large cat with glass eyes, then General McPherson of Civil War fame and a magnificent lion. At the end of the road was President Garfield standing in front of another abandoned house, his head nearly hidden by the limbs of a huge pine tree. I found Ulysses S. Grant in a clearing and George Washington in the woods. There was a WWI soldier standing at attention and a statue of General Sherman with no head. It was a day of unexpected discoveries and one that I won't soon forget.

Since that day I have visited Baughman Park many times and I'm still amazed by what I see there. Ten large statues of presidents and soldiers stand guard on the hillside. Numerous smaller carvings inhabit the rock outcrops. All the carvings were done by one remarkable man

Preface

named Brice Baughman. With only mallet and chisel, he chipped these monuments from native stone. He was self-taught and even forged his own tools. For forty years he carved stone, not for money or fame, but for the pleasure of creating monuments to men he respected. Brice once referred fondly to the "big moss-covered rocks asleep down in the quarry." *Thanks, Brice, for waking them!*

The statues in Baughman Park are genuine historic treasures. For decades their sightless eyes have gazed out over the wide valley below. They have stood perfectly still, unchanging, while the outside world has moved on and gradually forgotten them. More than a century has passed now since Brice Baughman first began creating his sculptures. During that time the tempo of our world has increased dramatically. We have gone from buggies to space ships. The little dirt road that once meandered across the valley below Baughman Hill is now a sweeping four-lane highway. Hundreds of cars, trucks and buses speed by everyday never knowing the unique place that lies just beyond the off-ramp.

Places like Baughman Park are important and must be preserved. They are landmarks in time – islands of history where things have remained relatively unchanged. It is in these places where we can reach out and touch the past. In the case of Baughman Park, it's not only the statues themselves that are important, it's also the legacy that Brice Baughman has created for future generations. In Brice Baughman's accomplishments we are shown our own potential. Here was a simple man who found a way to create something from nothing. What he created still inspires us today. A congressman who once visited Baughman Park wrote: "Most of us would have passed by these stones, but Brice Baughman saw in them the opportunity to make some of our great men and soldiers live in the minds and hearts of our people." This is the legacy of Brice Baughman and his park.

Many years ago Baughman Park was a popular place to picnic, attend social functions, hold family reunions and enjoy beautiful scenery among gleaming white monuments. Now, the park is largely unknown by the general public. Weeds and brush have taken over and the statues are gray and flaking. Vandalism has taken its toll. But the park still could have a bright future if the county, state or some philanthropic organization were to purchase it and restore it for the community. Baughman Park is an historic landmark like no other. No one can gaze at Brice's statues without feeling a sense of awe. He left us something very special – young and old alike are stirred by his vision.

Though the future of Baughman Park is uncertain, its past remains alive in the memories of many local folks. Some of them have forgotten the name of the park – but they will never forget the "Statues on the Hill."

The Sculptor

Daniel Brice Baughman
1874-1954

As a young boy, Brice Baughman began carving the stone on the hill where he lived in Muskingum County, Ohio. He had no carving tools, so he made his own. He had no training, yet he created masterpieces.

Brice was a kind and gentle man, loved and respected by all. He served the community for many years as an undertaker, but his passion was carving stone. Today, when we marvel at his achievements, we are enriched by his vision.

A Dedication from the Past

THERE is a charm and thrill about jotting down these few words, and as they unfold, my heart warms toward those people whom have spoken well of my park. The finest thoughts the human mind can cherish are possessed by me for you, my people.

On several occasions I have been tendered tribute of praise for my work: carving statues of the nation's celebrated dead. I assure you it was a labor of immense interest to me. I received early recognition by the public and the dedication given each statue is a source of increasing satisfaction.

When I look about me, my eyes rest upon the little white cottage where I lived my childhood, under loving care and tender guidance of noble parents; my good and loyal wife; the two sons; the stately oaks in the nearby woodland; the big moss-covered rocks asleep down in the quarry; the sublime view of the majestic valley – and my friends, I raise my eyes toward the Temple of Love and Solace, and offer silent supplication. I fully realize that the loveliest and most endearing memories of my life are centered here on the summit of the Baughman hills.

It behooves me at this time to extend my thanks to the kind and generous people, who, in any way contributed to this little book, for without their co-operation it could not have hoped to materialize.

Folks, I dedicate this book to you, and trust you find it worthy of a place in your keeping.

Very truly yours,

Daniel Brice Baughman

The letter above is copied from a souvenir booklet printed in 1931 for the official dedication of Baughman Memorial Park.

INTRODUCTION

Statues on the Hill

*O*hio's attic is full of history. It holds countless trunks and boxes packed with memories from our state's past. Everything is in there, from old mastodon bones to this morning's newspaper, but it's a dimly-lit place full of cobwebs and dust. Things have become buried under decades of clutter, others sit unnoticed in dark corners. Historical events, people and places that once were foremost in the minds of all Ohioans have gradually faded from our collective memory. This is the story of one of those forgotten places.

An Undertaker's Hobby

If you've never heard of Baughman Park, you're not alone. It was a well-known place during the 1920's, 30's and 40's, but since that time its fame has dwindled. Today, many younger people living within only a few miles of the park are unaware of its existence. Even some older folks in the area who remember the park from their childhood don't realize that it's still there, just hidden by the trees.

Baughman Park is located on a wooded hilltop in a rural part of Muskingum County, Ohio. The hill itself is not unusual, but what's on the hill is. On this hill stand several larger-than-life statues of U. S. Presidents and military leaders carved from the native sandstone. There are numerous other carvings in the stone outcrops along the hillside as well. All of these carvings were made between the 1880's and the late 1920's. They were all carved by one man – Daniel Brice Baughman.

Known by all as "Brice," Mr.. Baughman was a local undertaker and well-known member of the Masons and other fraternal organizations. Brice made his living as an undertaker but his hobby was carving stone. He was not formally trained in stone carving or any other arts, but he seemed to have a natural talent as a sculptor. As a boy he carved faces and other figures into the stone outcrops on the hill. Starting in early adulthood he began to carve free-standing statues of famous men.

Above: Statue of Abraham Lincoln in Baughman Park. The old house was the home of Noah Baughman, father of the sculptor.
(A. Keirns photo '00)

Opposite: Photo montage of the Ulysses S. Grant statue.
(A. Keirns photo illustration)

The National Register

Baughman Memorial Park is listed in the National Register of Historic Places. This listing does not protect the property, but it does offer the owner incentives to preserve and restore it.

A Park Takes Shape

All of the carvings Brice made were located on his father's farm. As the years went by and Brice's statues multiplied, the farm began to draw curious visitors from the surrounding counties. Brice created picnic areas to accommodate the visitors. He even built bleachers and a speakers' platform as the hill became more and more popular for family reunions, church services and other group meetings.

Baughman's hill was quickly turning into Baughman Park. Folks came from all over the state to picnic and marvel at the statues Brice had created. Somewhere along the way Brice began to think of the hill as a memorial. In 1931, the Governor of Ohio, Vic Donahey, made it official and honored Brice Baughman's work by dedicating the hill as "Baughman Memorial Park."

For many years the park was open to all. Brice never charged admission or asked for any payment for use of the park. Baughman Memorial Park was his gift to the people of Ohio, and the nation.

Eventually Brice grew too old to take care of the park and moved off the hill into nearby Dresden. The park sat idle for several years before being sold to a family who developed it into a camp ground. The next owners turned it into a private religious retreat for troubled teens. A few years later the land changed hands again. During these later years the park became overgrown and suffered vandalism. As time passed, the park was visited less and less by the public. Finally, in 1997, the land was purchased by The Longaberger Company.

The Longaberger Company

During the last few years, the sleepy area around Baughman Park has changed dramatically. Much of this change is the result of the growth of The Longaberger Company, started in the 1970's in nearby Dresden. Longaberger is a huge family-owned business known primarily as the country's largest manufacturer of high-quality, handmade baskets.

The Longaberger Company has purchased thousands of acres of land along State Route 16 to allow for future expansion and development. Their sprawling manufacturing campus east of Frazeysburg now employs several thousand people. The Longaberger Homestead, a family-oriented theme destination also located at the manufacturing campus, is becoming a popular tourist attraction. It's not unusual to see several hundred cars and dozens of tour buses parked at the Homestead every day during the peak seasons.

The tremendous growth of The Longaberger Company is drawing more and more people into this rural area. State Route 16 has been expanded into a four-lane highway to help ease the traffic congestion brought on by this influx of people and vehicles. Until a few short years ago, the intersection of State Routes 586 and 16 at the bottom of Baughman's hill

Above: An old postcard commemorating the dedication of the statue of President Harding in 1927.

Above: A stone lion rests near the statue of Civil War general, James B. McPherson.

(A. Keirns photo '00)

consisted of a stop sign and a small grocery store/restaurant known as "Aunt B's." Now the stop sign and Aunt B's are gone, replaced by a large concrete overpass with ramps leading down onto the new highway.

In 1997 Dave Longaberger, founder of The Longaberger Company, purchased the property on which Baughman Park is located. Dave, who passed away in 1999, was fascinated by the statues and the history of the park and bought it, in part, to protect it. The Longaberger Company has not changed or developed the park. At present it remains much as it was when Dave bought it. The main difference now is that it's a restricted area with a locked gate. Although this keeps the general public out, it also reduces the likelihood of vandalism which has been a serious problem over the years. The Longaberger Company's future plans for the park have not been made public.

The Story Continues

Baughman Park is not gone, it's just hiding. Most of the monuments Brice Baughman carved are still intact. The statues aren't gleaming white as they once were, and the grounds aren't manicured, but Brice's vision of a memorial park still stands on his hill.

The purpose of this book is to reacquaint Ohioans with a unique historic treasure that exists in their state. It's been more than 75 years since Baughman Memorial Park's official dedication in 1931. By keeping the memory of the park alive, we honor not only Brice Baughman but also the presidents and soldiers he memorialized in stone.

Welcome to the story of the Statues on the Hill…

Below: The Baughman family poses in their Buick in front of the Doughboy in 1921.

Left to right: Brice Baughman in his Commandry uniform; Brice's father Noah; Hubert Claypool; Harold "Jabbo" Baughman; Brice's wife Bessie; and Lester Baughman.

Later, this Buick was converted into a hearse for the funeral business.

(Photo Courtesy of Ray Murray)

CHAPTER ONE

A Hill of Stone

Above: View of the quarry at Baughman Park.

(A. Keirns photo '01)

Brice Baughman may never have picked up a mallet and chisel had he not grown up on a hill made of stone. It was this hill that helped determine his destiny. Brice spent his life shaping stone, and all the while the stone was shaping him. The story of Baughman Park has to begin with a little history of the stone itself, for without it there would be no story to tell.

Sandstone

Baughman Park is located on a hill in the northwest corner of Muskingum County, Ohio, about fifteen miles east of Newark. It's an area of rugged beauty with numerous sandstone cliffs, ledges and outcrops of various shapes and sizes.

Sandstone is a sedimentary rock formed over millions of years as water-deposited sediments become compressed and solidified. The stone exposed in Baughman Park is likely a Pennsylvanian-age sandstone of the upper Pottsville Group, possibly the *Homewood* sandstone. Homewood sandstone has been described as "fine-grained with well-rounded quartz grains, micaceous in part and cross-bedded." This identification is somewhat speculative, however, due to the complexity of the Pennsylvanian stratigraphy in Ohio.

Sandstone is a porous rock with a high silica content. When cut up into blocks it makes a strong material for foundations and bridges. During Ohio's canal period sandstone from this area was used extensively in building locks and culverts. Later, during the railroad-building period, it was used for railroad bridge abutments and was also pulverized to make glass. In the area around Baughman Park, sandstone appears in a range of colors from light brown to red-orange. It tends to darken when exposed to the elements, often becoming dark gray or black. Brice Baughman's statues would be very dark in color were it not for the fact that he painted them white.

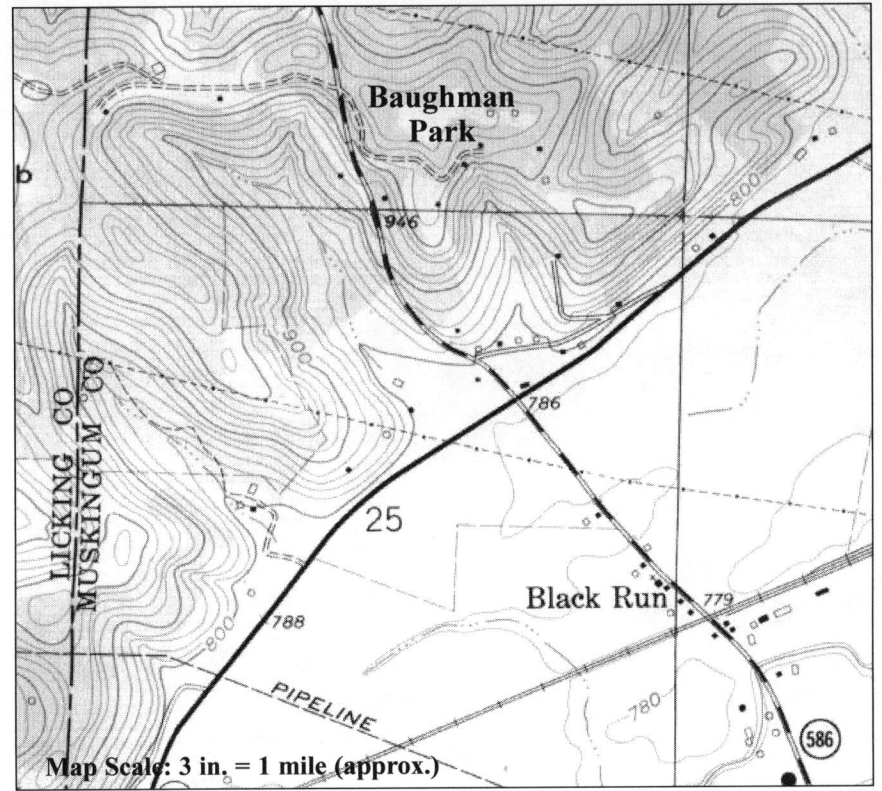

Left: Baughman Park overlooks a wide valley which curves east through Frazeysburg and north to Coshocton. According to geologists, this valley was cut by the prehistoric Newark River. (This topo map does not show the new path of State Route 16).

Above: Baughman Park (represented by the black dot) lies just outside the glaciated area of the state.

THE ADVANCE OF THE GLACIERS

Millions of years after the sandstone formed, the climate gradually cooled and we entered what geologists call the *Ice Age*. During this period, much of Ohio's landscape was forever changed as massive glaciers plowed into the state from the north. These mile-thick sheets of ice were slow but powerful, moving earth and rock like gigantic bulldozers. They rounded off high spots and filled in the low areas. Rocks were picked up from a variety of sources and carried along or ground up into soil. As the glaciers melted they deposited this mixture, many feet deep in some places, covering the old sedimentary deposits.

Fortunately for Brice Baughman the glaciers didn't scour the entire area we now call Ohio. They advanced and retreated several times but the southeastern quarter of the state remained virtually untouched. Baughman Park sits along the edge of this glacial boundary just outside the glaciated area. The landscape here is older and rugged, cut up by streams and marked by steep valleys and narrow ridges. It's here, where the glaciers didn't reach, that the old sandstone deposits still lie at the surface. Brice didn't need to dig to find stone to carve, it was right under his feet.

CHAPTER TWO

A Boy Inspired

In 1879, Noah and Sarah Baughman purchased forty-two acres known as Bald Hill. They paid $1000 dollars for the land (a little under $24 per acre). Their son, Brice, was five years old when they moved up to the hill. The rocky hill wasn't the best farmland but Noah managed to grow some crops and raise a few animals. Young Brice enjoyed living on the rugged hill from the very beginning. Like most boys, he liked to play on the rocks and ledges protruding from the hillside. The view was spectacular too. From the top of his hill Brice could see into four counties: Muskingum, Licking, Coshocton and Knox.

As Brice played among the rocks, he began to see something that no one else seemed to notice. Like a potter who looks at a lump of clay and sees the beautiful vase it will become, Brice saw the potential of the stone and was inspired by it.

The Quarry Years

While Brice was growing up, he learned farming from his father. "Grandad always had such nice horses, sheep and pigs," remembers Lester Baughman, Brice's eldest son. Later, Noah found a way to add extra income to his farm by taking advantage of his endless supply of sandstone.

According to local history, Noah Baughman opened a quarrying operation on the hill in 1898. It's likely that some quarrying had been going on even before that date. Good building stone was in high demand and Baughman's hill had plenty. For several years the quarry prospered, shipping as many as 200 train-car loads of stone per year, much of it destined for railroad bridges and road beds. A large part of this business came when the Panhandle division of the Pennsylvania Railroad laid a double-track line from Columbus to Pittsburgh. Stone from Noah's quarry was also used in the glass making industry. According to a short biography of Noah in a Muskingum County history book: "…this branch of his business [the quarry] adds not a little to his income."

Above: What may be one of Brice's earliest attempts at carving a human figure, stares out from a ledge on the side of the hill.

Opposite: In an early carving of Abraham Lincoln, Brice captured a pensive mood. Like many of the carvings in Baughman Park, this one has been vandalized and is missing part of the nose.

(A. Keirns photos '01)

17

Black Run

The area around Baughman Park has always been sparsely populated. Today the closest town of any size is Frazeysburg three miles to the east. Baughman Park is usually referred to as being located at Black Run.

During the early 1900's Black Run was a flourishing village located where the Pennsylvania Railroad crosses State Rt. 586 just south of Baughman Park. It had a train depot, two stores, its own post office and several houses.

Today, Black Run consists of a small cluster of homes and other buildings at the south end of the State Route 16 overpass. There is also a small creek here called Black Run from which the village takes its name.

Like many small communities, Black Run also had a one-room school building. Black Run School was located outside of the village along the north side of old State Rt. 16, near the eastern end of Baughman's hill.

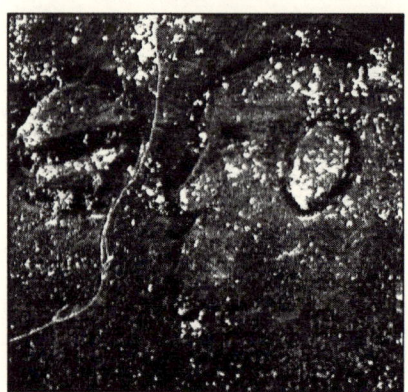

Above: Nearly hidden along a low ledge is what appears to be a very early attempt by Brice to carve the profile of a face.
(A. Keirns photo '01)

It was apparently in this quarry that young Brice first learned to work with stone. In helping his father in the quarry and watching the other quarry workers, he gained valuable experience. He learned how the stone was drilled, removed, shaped, lifted and transported. These skills would serve him well when he started creating his statues later on.

Quarrying was hard work. Brice could have easily developed a strong dislike for working with stone, but instead, he was fascinated by it. During his free time he would sit along the rocky ledges pecking away at the stone for hours until recognizable shapes began to slowly emerge.

It's likely that the natural shape of some outcrops suggested subjects to Brice. He worked the stone with whatever tools he could find or make. As one newspaper report would later state: "He exhibited unusual patience, making his own sculpturing chisels from whatever abandoned piece of farm machinery he could utilize for this purpose."

It was during these early years that Brice carved a variety of faces and other figures into the outcrops along the south side of the hill. With each new carving he learned a little more and got a little better.

There is nothing easy about carving stone. It's an unforgiving medium. It must have been tedious and frustrating for the young Brice. His tools were crude and the stone was not the best for carving. After all, this wasn't fine Italian marble, this was Ohio sandstone which had been exposed to the elements for centuries. In some places it was hard and grainy, in others it was soft and friable. It often had inclusions, cracks and other flaws and was unpredictable at best. Most boys would have given up and found a less demanding pastime, but not Brice. Something inside of him was driving him on.

AN ECLECTIC MENAGERIE

Brice's carvings were crude at first, stiff and lifeless. But right from the start he seems to have had a desire to carve subjects with symbolic significance. He didn't go for classical scrollwork or floral designs, instead, he tried to carve life into the stone. The ledges along the south side of the hill are alive with Brice's early work.

It's impossible to determine the chronological order in which these early carvings were made. They seem to be randomly placed along the hillside. Some are significantly better than others, but there is no discernible pattern that would indicate that Brice started at one end of the hill and worked toward the other end. Most likely he chose a particular spot to make a carving based on the natural shape of the outcrop and the shape of the subject he had in mind.

A variety of faces gaze out from the rocks, some recognizable, some less so. A man with a top hat, a horse head with a curving neck, an eagle, antlers from a missing deer head, an Indian with raised tomahawk and a small depiction of Jesus on the cross. There's also an area often referred

Above: Heavily vandalized carving of a womens' rights suffragist holding a scroll.
(A. Keirns photo '01)

Left: The same sculpture as it looked when Brice first carved it. The scroll read: "VOTE FOR…(Women?) The final word is difficult to make out. Note the eagle wings at the right of the picture.
(Courtesy of Ray Murray)

to as the "Republican Corner" which includes an elephant head, a bust of President Taft (now headless), an inscribed stone column and some Masonic symbols among other things.

Many of the carvings here could be characterized as *bas-relief*, they project from the surface but have no undercutting. Others however show a pronounced projection with deep undercutting and are much more three-dimensional.

As can be seen by the photographs in this chapter, some of these carvings are more distinct than others. Several have been heavily damaged by vandalism, especially by bullets. Some are discolored and covered with lichens or moss. All have been exposed to decades of weathering which has eroded their once-distinct features.

Reference

In order for Brice to capture the likeness of an individual, he would need references to work from. It's likely that Brice used a variety of sources as reference material. He may have used a combination of newspapers, magazines, books and possibly images obtained through his association with veterans' organizations, the Masons, Elks, and others. Some of his subjects were even pictured on U. S. currency.

On at least one occasion, Brice's wife, Bessie, reluctantly served as a model for one of the statues. Lester Baughman, Brice's son, remembers his mother posing for Brice as he worked on the Roosevelt statue: "Roosevelt was large and so was Mother, so she put on Dad's coat and stood there while he carved Roosevelt's coat."

It's possible that Brice made preliminary sketches or drawings of his subjects before carving them, but so far, none of these have turned up.

The Accidental Undertaker

According to local lore, Brice Baughman became an undertaker by accident. As the story goes, an undertaker from a neighboring town came to Brice with a plea for help. The man owed $100 to a coffin factory and

Above: Although now damaged by vandals, early references to this figure describe it as a woman with raised arms. This figure may have been another suffragist. (Suffrage is an old term that essentially means "the right to vote").

The women's rights movement, especially the right to vote, was a volatile issue during the early 1900's. Finally in 1919, Congress passed the 19th Amendment to the Constitution, stating that no citizen could be denied the right to vote "on account of sex."
(A. Keirns photos '01)

19

Right: Brice in his later years with his horse-drawn hearse and the old coffin he kept inside. He often invited visitors to lift the lid of the coffin and take a look. When they did, they would find themselves face to face with a skeleton. "Most women shriek in horror," Brice once confided.
(Photo courtesy of Lester Baughman)

Above: Christ on the cross.

Below: Benjamin Franklin?
(A. Keirns photos '01)

couldn't make the payment. Brice advanced the undertaker the money and received a horse-drawn hearse in return. "That put the stone-dealer in the undertaking business...," stated a 1942 article in the Zanesville Times-Signal.

The same newspaper article also said that the man to whom Brice loaned the money soon became Brice's embalmer. A year later the embalmer left and Brice was "...obliged to learn that trade."

Brice's son, Lester, says that his father did attend schooling to become an embalmer. Brice went to Columbus for the schooling which lasted about six weeks. While attending the school he was able to pick up a few carving tips by watching an experienced sculptor who was carving figures to adorn a park gate near where he was living.

THE FUNERAL BUSINESS

Brice began his undertaking business in 1902. Whether it was by accident or by design, it seemed to suit him well. By all accounts, Brice was a man who liked to be around people, and he was well-liked in return. As an undertaker he became known to just about everyone in the area. This gave him the opportunity to visit and talk with people on a more regular basis.

"He loved people," recalls Brice's son, Lester. "He was also quite a story teller." Lester says his father didn't like to see people sad and would try to cheer them up with his stories.

Brice was "...famous as a tobacco chewer and a great raconteur," quipped a fellow funeral director from nearby Zanesville. Brice would often go outside during a funeral to have a chew and would usually strike up a conversation with someone. It wouldn't be long before he would be surrounded by people listening to him talk, chew, tell stories and, of course, occasionally spit.

Above: Ohioan, William Howard Taft, U. S. President 1909-1913.

Top Left: An early photo of the outcrop known as "Republican Corner." William H. Taft is shown with right hand raised. The elephant is a symbol of the Republican Party as are the letters "G.O.P." which stand for the "Grand Old Party."
(Courtesy of Curtis "Bud" Abbott)

Left: The Republican Corner as it looks today. At the far left are the remains of the suffragist with scroll and a headless eagle.
(A. Keirns photo '00)

Taft Laughed

According to a 1952 newspaper article in the Newark Advocate:

"Brice carved a likeness of William Howard Taft and, just to make it different, he posed the statesman with his hand on the Bible as in an inauguration scene, even though Taft had not yet been elected president. Then, after Taft did become president some jokester broke off the hand and book! Because of this odd coincidence, Brice sent a picture of the broken statue to the president. In a very cordial reply, the chief executive indicated that he, too, had enjoyed a good laugh from the incident."

The article refers to the carving of Taft in the Republican Corner. Although Taft's right arm is raised as if he were taking an oath, there is no visible indication of a Bible.

Brice also had a keen sense of humor and was an astute observer of politics. He was an ardent Republican which is evidenced by the Presidents he chose to memorialize. However, Brice was "not a rabid partisan when it comes to politics," said one newspaper report.

One of the things Brice liked about the undertaking business was that it brought in an income but didn't take up all of his time. This was a rural community and he was seldom overwhelmed with business. In between funerals he found plenty of time to pursue his hobby – stone carving. This suited him just fine. Brice did well in the funeral business and also continued to help his father run the stone quarry until about 1914.

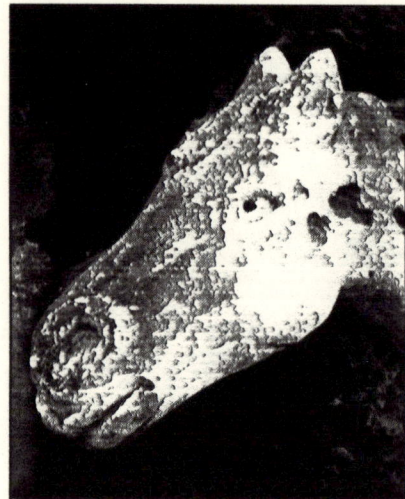

Above: Detail of horse head. The holes to the right of the eye are bullet holes made by vandals.

Top Right: A large rock just east of the Republican Corner includes a child (or cherub?), horse head, antlers from a missing deer head, and what appears to be the remains of a ram's head with curved horns.

(A. Keirns photos '01)

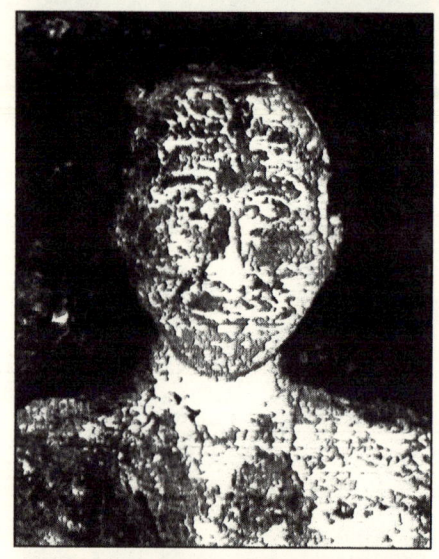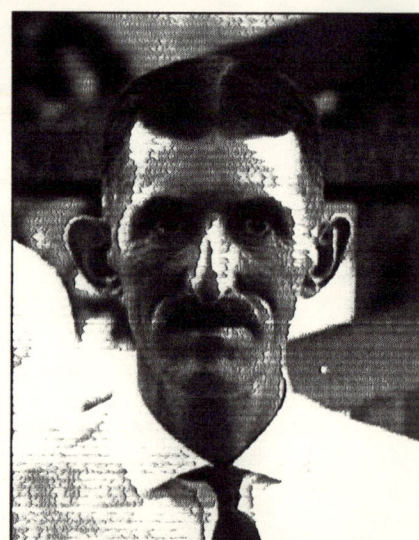

Right: We know that Brice liked to portray real people in his carvings. We don't know for sure who these two carvings are meant to portray, but they bear a strong resemblance to the photographs to their right. That's Brice at the top and his father, Noah, on the bottom. Could it be?

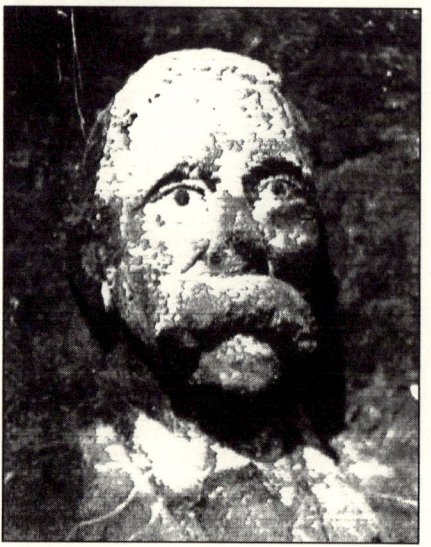

Above: Detail of the Indian.

Top Left: In this grouping we see Abe Lincoln on the far left, then the remains of a bare-breasted woman, an Indian with tomahawk and what may be a portrait of Rutherford B. Hayes on the far right. Hayes was an Ohioan who served as President of the United States from 1877 to 1881. Also, note the date "1911" visible near the raised elbow of the Indian.
(A. Keirns photo '94)

Left: Close-up of bearded man from top photo compared to a photograph of President Hayes.

Below: The defaced sculpture of a black man eating watermelon, a demeaning but common racial image of the time. This carving, along with the bare-breasted woman mentioned above, were considered offensive and were destroyed when the park was owned by a church group.

BRICE BEGINS A FAMILY

Brice married Bessie Lindemood in 1914 at the age of 39. Their marriage produced two sons: Lester in 1915 and Harold in 1917. The couple also raised Brice's young nephew, Hubert Claypool.

As Lester and his younger brother Harold grew, they both helped their father in the undertaking business. Lester would sometimes skip school in order to help his father when he was short-handed.

Lester recalls that his father would sometimes get "death calls" late at night. Brice would have to get up, hitch the horse to the buggy and head down the dark road. Traveling on rutted dirt roads in a one-horsepower buggy was a slow process and there was no time to waste when a body was waiting to be embalmed.

Getting the horse hitched-up in the middle of the night was not always

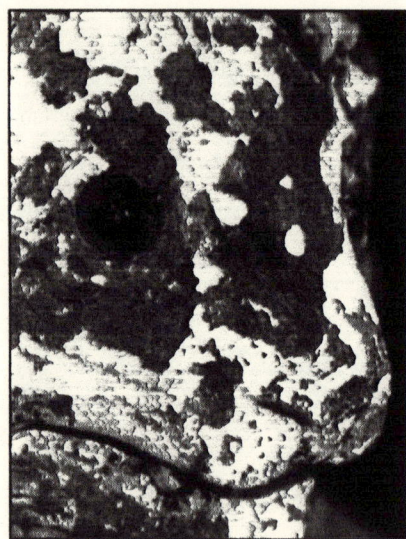

Above and Right: This large cat lies a few yards west of the McPherson statue. Although it resembles a house cat, it's much larger than a domestic feline. It has also been called a cougar or panther. Close-up photo above shows the cat's glass eyes.
(A. Keirns photos '98)

Above: An odd character (clown?) smiles at visitors from a large rock near the McKinley statue.
(A. Keirns photos '01)

Right: Old service booklet from Brice's funeral business, a poignant memento of the 1911 funeral of a young child from Frazeysburg.

Three phone numbers are shown on the cover: Bell Phone 86 K1, Farmers Phone 618, and citizens Phone-- Black Run.
(Courtesy of Ray Murray)

easy, however. "Sometimes that horse would run from Dad and he'd have to chase it around the field," recalls Lester with a chuckle.

In those days funerals were held in the home or sometimes in a church. The embalmer brought the necessary equipment and embalmed the body right on site. Eventually funeral parlors (also called funeral homes) became more common. Brice transformed a barn on his hill into a funeral home which served the community for several years. Later this building was remodeled and used as a private residence.

Both Lester and Harold Baughman went on to make their careers in the funeral business, taking over where their father left off.

Top Left: The Lion has always been a favorite location for snapshots. It was also a great place for a dapper gentleman to show-off his stylish button shoes!
(Courtesy of Chance Brockway)

Center Left: The Lion has been the delight of generations of children visiting the park. Many old snapshots show kids "riding" the king of the jungle, although some children were afraid to approach the great stone beast. In this snapshot, (L to R) Myrna & Rena Steele and Dorothy & Carrie Spitzer ride the Lion, ca. 1928.
(Courtesy of Rena Steele Abbott)

Bottom Left: The Lion as it looks today. Like the Cat sculpture, the Lion also has glass eyes.

The Lion lies just east of the McPherson statue. According to local lore, there was a large outcrop of stone here just begging to be carved. A druggist from Zanesville, Mr. C. A. Baird, suggested to Brice that the shape of the outcrop resembled a lion. Brice agreed. In 1915 he carved a majestic lion from the outcrop. To thank Mr. Baird for his suggestion, Brice carved his name prominently on the front of the sculpture.

Above: A mysterious man in a top hat looks out from his shady ledge on the hillside near the McPherson statue. This carving probably represents a real person, but who?
(A. Keirns photo '94)

25

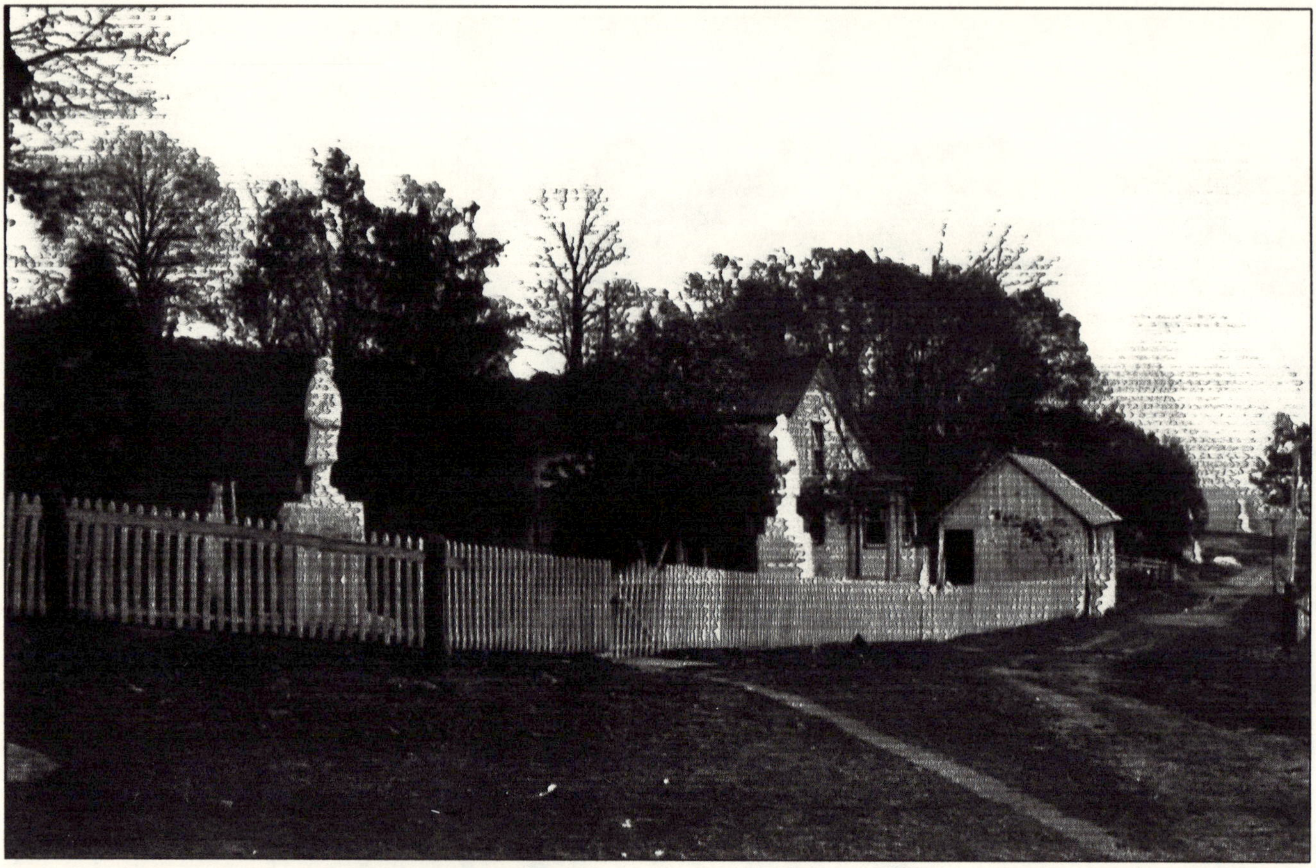

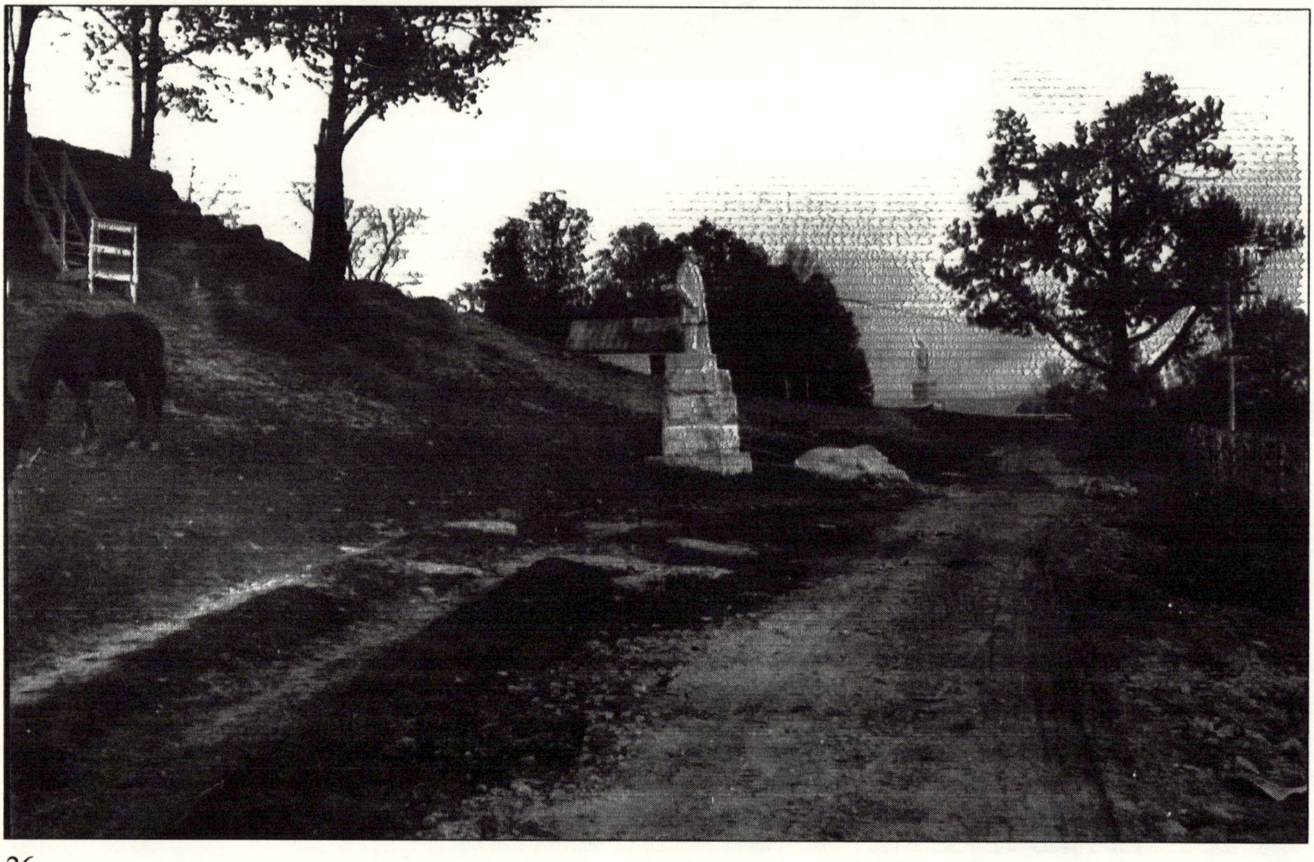

Far Left Top: Old view of Noah Baughman's house (looking east) sometime after 1915. Five sculptures are visible: (left to right) McKinley, Lincoln, McPherson, Lion and Garfield.
(Collection of Chance Brockway)

Left: More recent view of Noah Baughman's house (Mar. 2000).
(A. Keirns photo '00)

Far Left Bottom: Old view of McPherson, the Lion and Garfield (looking east) sometime after 1915. House beyond McPherson statue is home of Brice Baughman.
(Collection of Chance Brockway)

Below: Same view as it appeared in Oct., 1998. Garage building has since been torn down and removed.
(A. Keirns photo '98)

CHAPTER THREE

STATUES RISE FROM THE QUARRY

Above: An old drill rod is still lodged in the stone at the top edge of the quarry where it became stuck many decades ago.

Below: Baughman Quarry.
(A. Keirns photos '01)

At some point during Brice Baughman's late teens or early 20's he decided to attempt a free-standing statue. This would be a much more demanding task than carving into an outcropping.

To make a statue he would first need to quarry out a large block of stone weighing several tons. The next challenge would be to carve an entire figure in full three-dimensional form or "in the round" as it's called in the art world. He would also need to prepare a substantial stone base on which the statue would stand. When the base was ready he would have to transport the statue to the site and raise it onto the base. This would take a tremendous amount of work and skill – but Brice was up to the task.

When we look at Brice's statues today, we see a finished product. It's easy to forget that they once were all just part of a huge mass of sandstone in Noah Baughman's quarry.

To really appreciate the magnitude of Brice's achievements, it's helpful to understand the process he had to go through to create a statue. There were variations in quarrying techniques utilized during the late 1800's and early 1900's, so we don't know the exact method Brice may have used to quarry his stone. It's likely, however, that the general process went something like the following:

DRILLING

First, Brice had to select a place in the quarry wall where he could remove a block of sandstone large enough for a statue. He had to examine the stone to make sure it didn't have cracks or other obvious faults. When he was satisfied with his choice, he would mark out the area he wanted and begin drilling holes down into the top of the quarry wall.

Drilling was a strenuous job. The driller held a pointed iron drill rod in one hand and slowly rotated it while striking it with a hammer. Another common technique was using a "jumper drill." With this method, one man held and rotated the drill by means of an attached horizontal handle, while another man repeatedly hit the end of the drill with a sledge hammer. Steam-powered and compressed-air drills did exist as early as the mid-1800's but it's not known whether Brice had access to such tools.

Several holes would be drilled to remove a large block. Often two sizes of holes were drilled, the smaller holes being about 3/4" in diameter, the larger holes up to 2-1/2" in diameter. The smaller holes were drilled about 4" to 6" apart, while the larger holes were drilled up to 16" apart. In sandstone, the depth of the holes would usually be about two-thirds of the thickness of the layer of rock to be removed.

PLUG AND FEATHERS

After all the necessary holes were drilled, a method known as "plug and feathers" was often utilized to remove the stone block. A plug was a long, tapered piece of wood which might be round or square in cross section. A feather was a malleable iron wedge which looked something like half of a tube cut lengthwise. Two feathers and one plug were placed into each hole. When all the plugs and feathers were in place, a large hammer was used to drive in the plugs. Starting at one end of the line of holes, each plug was struck in succession, continuing to the other end. As this process was repeated, the pressure against the stone gradually increased. Eventually, the pressure became so great that the stone block broke away along the line of holes and fell into the quarry bed.

In some cases, an explosive such as blasting powder or dynamite was put into the holes and detonated, instead of using plugs and feathers.

DERRICKS, STONE BOATS AND SLEDS

Brice now had a huge block of sandstone weighing several tons lying in the quarry. In order to move and maneuver the block he would need to use a "derrick." A derrick is a simple machine consisting of a tall mast, and a moveable arm with ropes and pulleys attached to a windlass. This type of lifting device has been used for centuries and is essentially a "block and tackle" suspended on a movable arm. Sizes of derricks varied depending on the weight of the load needing to be lifted. There were also portable derricks that were used to set stones in place at a building site.

The next step for Brice would be to square-off the base, set the stone upright and begin roughing out the general shape of the statue. Brice would have used a variety of hammers, picks and chisels for this process. Judging by old photographs of statues in the quarry, Brice carved the statues to almost final form while still in the quarry. This process took many months or even years working part-time. Sometimes a statue would sit untouched for weeks or months during periods of harsh weather.

Brice also had to prepare a base for his statue to sit on. His bases usually consisted of three or four large blocks of sandstone stacked on top of one another. First he would prepare a level spot for the base, which might include digging into the ground and shaping the underlying stone

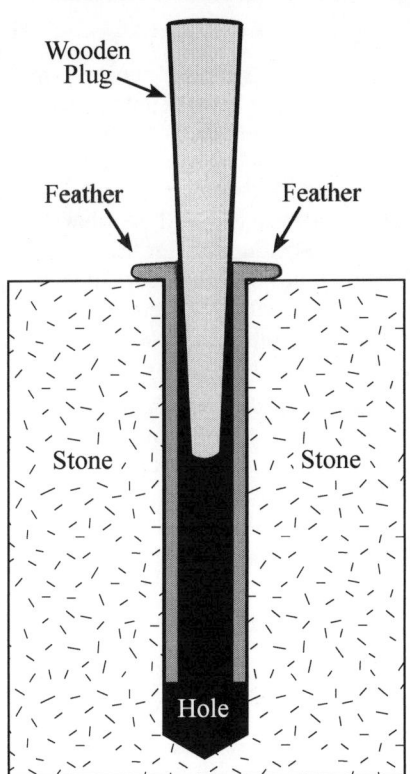

Above: Cross-section diagram showing a drill hole with plug and feathers inserted. As the tapered plug is driven further into the hole, it exerts increasing pressure against the feathers, eventually cracking the stone.

Above: In this old view of the Harding statue in the quarry, the tall mast of Brice's derrick is visible with its windlass at the bottom.

(Photo courtesy of Ray Murray)

Folk Art

Art is a slippery concept. In school we all learn about the great artists of the world, painters and sculptors who are considered masters of their craft. Many of their names are still familiar to us even centuries after they lived. Sometimes our knowledge of what is considered "great" art interferes with our ability to recognize other wonderful art when we see it.

Some of the best art ever created is done by children with crayons and paper. It's unassuming, highly expressive and touches us on a level Michelangelo couldn't begin to reach. Yet, you won't find this art framed and hanging in the Louvre.

We tend to separate art into categories such as fine art, graphic art, folk art, and so on. This categorization is handy for teaching or learning about art, but it shouldn't be confused with a hierarchy. One category of art is not better or worse than another any more than the color blue is better or worse than the color red.

Brice Baughman's art is categorized as "folk art." One definition of folk art is: "a reflection, not of formal training, but of an artist's personalized world view and creation spirit." The qualifying factor here seems to be the lack of formal training. The term folk art is not derogatory. It is simply an artificial designation used to classify art created by a self-taught individual. Folk artists are often unaware of the classical rules of art, yet they create wonderful works. Like children's art, folk art has not been molded or homogenized by formal training and remains the pure expression of an individual.

Folk art is rarely as monumental as the statues created by Brice Baughman. His work takes folk art to a new level. If any place could be considered the Mt. Rushmore of folk art, Baughman Park is it.

---

surface. The heavy base blocks would be pulled to the site by horses using a "stone boat" or sled which was simply a wooden skid dragged along the ground. The blocks would then be lifted into position by the derrick.

It's likely that Brice moved the statue to the site using the same method as the base blocks. Once the derrick was set up at the site, he probably set the base blocks and the statue before dismantling the derrick.

After the statue was in place, Brice constructed a wooden scaffold around the statue on which he could stand. This is where he would put the finishing touches on his sculpture with mallet and chisel, often getting down to look up at the statue from ground level.

Painting

When Brice was satisfied with the final results, he painted his statue white. He used a special mixture made from house paint which was designed to seal the statues against the weather. Brice was quick to point out that his statues were coated in real paint, not whitewash. The gleaming white color also enhanced the look of the statue, making it look more like traditional statuary which was usually carved in white marble.

Inscriptions

It's evident from old photographs that Brice carved the inscriptions and dates into his statues sometime after they were finished. This may have been months or even years later in some cases. The inscriptions were a tricky part of the sculpture for Brice.

"Sometimes Dad had trouble with his letters," recalls Brice's son, Lester. A close look at some of the inscriptions on the statues reveals misspellings and a few reversed letters here and there. We find it very unusual to see a misspelled word on a monumental stone sculpture, but then, Baughman Park is an unusual place – and that's part of its charm.

Presidents and Soldiers

Brice Baughman put a lot of thought into each figure he chose to carve. He liked to memorialize fellow Ohioans. He carved a total of ten free-standing statues: six presidents and four soldiers (although one soldier could be counted as a President). Of the six presidents, three were from Ohio: McKinley, Garfield and Harding. The soldiers, Grant, McPherson and Sherman were also Ohioans. The fourth soldier, the Doughboy, was symbolic and didn't represent any individual. All told, Brice carved six Ohioans, three non-Ohioans and one symbolic figure.

Brice was a Republican and his party choice is evident in the Presidents he chose to memorialize. There are no Democrats standing on Baughman Hill. Although, in all fairness, Brice did have plans to carve at least two Democrats: President Woodrow Wilson and Ohio Governor Vic Donahey, but these statues were never done.

CHRONOLOGY

As far as we know, Brice didn't leave us any written records about his statues. We believe that the first statue he carved was McKinley around 1898 and his last was Harding in 1927, but it's difficult to assign a definite chronological sequence to his work.

Each statue in **Baughman Park was dedicated to a particular organization** and, at some point, a dedication ceremony was held. The date of the dedication has often been used as a reference in trying to determine the sequence in which Brice carved his statues. Unfortunately, this method of dating may not be very accurate.

Various sources differ in their account of how long it took Brice to create a statue. Some say one year, others say two, three or even four years. The actual length of time was probably somewhere in between those estimates and no doubt varied for each statue. To complicate matters further, there are photographs showing the statues of Roosevelt and Harding standing side by side in the quarry. This indicates that Brice may have worked on more than one statue at a time.

Evidence also suggests that Brice may have finished some of his statues months or even years before they were officially dedicated. It appears that he carved the dedication date and other information on the statues *after* the dedication ceremony. We know, that at least in one case, two statues (McPherson and Garfield) were both dedicated on the same day.

There does appear to be somewhat of a pattern in the order Brice placed the statues on the grounds of Baughman Park. Generally speaking, he seems to have placed the statues in a counter-clockwise order, beginning with McKinley and ending with Harding.

Brice put McKinley and Lincoln in the front yard of his father's house, suggesting that Lincoln may have been the second statue he finished. Then it appears he continued to move east toward his own house, with McPherson and Garfield. He then moved slightly up the hill with Grant and on to the top of the hill with Washington. He moved toward the west with The Doughboy and Sherman (although the Sherman statue was dedicated before The Doughboy). Brice continued west with Roosevelt and finally Harding. When visitors drive into Baughman Park from State Route 586, the first statue they see is the last statue Brice carved.

THE STATUES

The following chapter shows all of the statues on Baughman Hill. Old photographs are reproduced wherever possible to show how the statues looked in their original condition. Information about the men Brice chose to memorialize is also included to help put the statues into context.

The statues are shown in the approximate order in which we believe Brice carved them, starting with McKinley and proceeding counter-clockwise to Harding.

Death Row

It's interesting that the three Presidents Brice placed along the road between his father's house and his own, were all victims of assassination. In addition, the one other figure in this row of statues, General McPherson, was also killed by a bullet. All of the other individuals depicted in the park died of natural causes.

We can speculate that Brice was deeply moved by McKinley's assassination in 1901. This incident may have prompted Brice to choose Lincoln, Garfield and McPherson as his next subjects.

Imperfect Perfection

It can't be ignored that there are some technical inaccuracies in Brice's work. There is a certain rigidity to his figures, some proportional problems and a tendency to carve rather large ears. A few misspellings can also be found here and there.

Technical inaccuracies are an inherent part of most folk art. They are like the seasonings in your grandmother's meatloaf. They reflect the personal taste, experience and ability of the cook. Her recipe comes from the heart, not from a cookbook. Brice's sculpture is like that, it isn't by the book – it's better.

CHAPTER FOUR

WILLIAM MCKINLEY

TWENTY-FIFTH PRESIDENT
1897-1901

Carving a recognizable likeness of a particular individual into a block of stone is difficult for even the most experienced sculptor. It would be much easier to carve a symbolic figure whose face wouldn't need to resemble a particular person. But Brice didn't take the easy way out. For his first statue he chose to carve the likeness of a well-known political figure, William McKinley.

PRESIDENT OR GOVERNOR?

The McKinley statue presents us with somewhat of a dilemma. Local lore says that Brice completed the statue of McKinley in 1898 and that it took him three years to carve this first statue. Over the years, several written articles have echoed this belief. If this is true, then Brice must have begun carving McKinley in 1895. The problem is, McKinley didn't serve as President until 1897.

Is it possible that Brice actually started carving McKinley *before* he was elected President? Surprisingly, the answer may be yes.

Before William McKinley became President, he was the Governor of Ohio. He held this office from 1892 to 1896. If Brice started carving McKinley in 1895, he wasn't memorializing a president, he was simply honoring his Governor. If it did take him three years to carve McKinley, the statue started out as a Governor and ended up as a President.

PRESIDENTIAL PROPORTIONS

The McKinley statue was Brice's first attempt at carving a complete figure. He carved McKinley approximately life-size. The overall proportions of this statue appear somewhat short and squat. On subsequent statues Brice achieved better results by making his statues larger and taller. He seems to have also discovered that a statue being viewed from below needs to be slightly elongated in order to counteract the visual effects of foreshortening.

Above: President McKinley.

Opposite: An early photo of the McKinley statue before the G. A. R. inscription was carved into the front.
(Photo Courtesy of Ray Murray)

Inscription on the Statue
(shown exactly as carved)

Front

WM MCKINLEY
PRES· 1897-1901

IN HONOR G.A.R.
ZANSVILLE

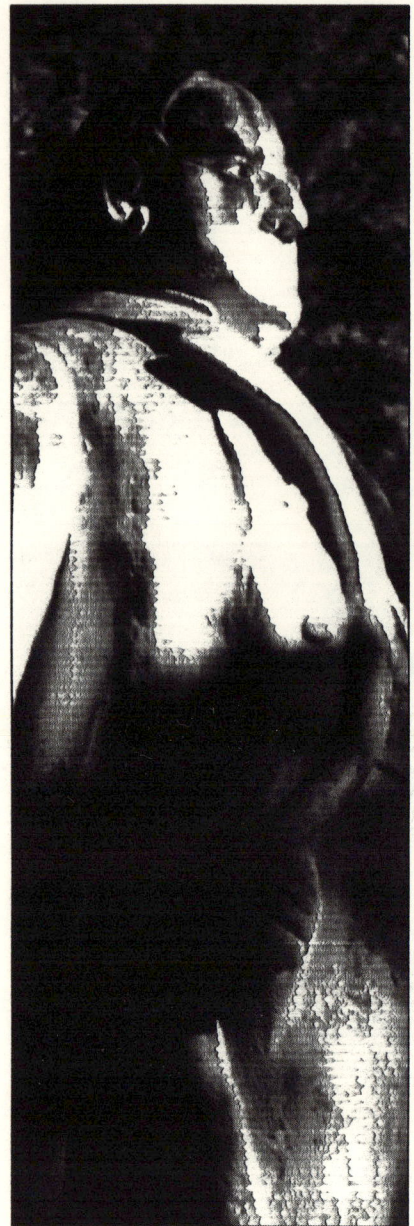

Above: Detail of McKinley.

Top Right: McKinley and Lincoln cast long shadows in the early morning sunlight.
(A. Keirns photos '98)

O cruel vile accursed blow –
That laid our loved McKinley low;
The world's great soul
is bowed with grief,
O Father! is there no relief?

Excerpted from "The Sorrow of the Nations," a poem by John P. Smith.

Highlights of McKinley's Life

William McKinley was born in Niles, Ohio, in 1843. In 1861 he enlisted as a private in an Ohio infantry regiment. Coincidentally, the regiment was commanded by a colonel who would later become President himself, Rutherford B. Hayes. McKinley participated in several battles and was promoted to the rank of brevet major. He would become the last Civil War veteran to be elected President.

After the war McKinley practiced law and established a practice in Canton. He served in the U. S. House of Representatives and later served as Governor of Ohio from 1892-96.

He was elected to the presidency in 1896 and took office in 1897. During his tenure as President, the United States declared war on Spain and invaded Cuba, Puerto Rico, Guam and the Philippines in what we now call the Spanish-American War. The invasion by land and sea quickly brought Spain to its knees. The resulting treaty gave Cuba its independence and granted Puerto Rico, Guam and the Philippines to the United States. McKinley also acquired Hawaii for the United States.

McKinley's popularity won him a second term as President. Speaking at the Pan-American Exposition in Buffalo, New York, McKinley said, "Isolation is no longer possible or desirable. The period of exclusiveness is past." The next day, an anarchist named Leon Czolgosz, shot the president. McKinley died eight days later on Sept. 14, 1901, thrusting Vice President, Theodore Roosevelt into the presidency.

Above: A huge pine tree nearly obscures McKinley's head.
(A. Keirns photo '94)

Top Left: McKinley in profile in Noah Baughman's front yard.
(Chance Brockway Collection)

Left: McKinley campaign pins.

35

ABRAHAM LINCOLN

SIXTEENTH PRESIDENT
1861-1865

Abraham Lincoln has become a national icon whose face is instantly recognizable even to young school children. He is also one of four American presidents to be assassinated.

Brice Baughman's decision to carve Lincoln may have resulted, in part, from McKinley's assassination. The first three presidents Brice carved were the three presidents that had been assassinated up to that point in time (the fourth, John F. Kennedy, was assassinated in 1963, long after Brice's death).

It's not certain that Lincoln was Brice's second statue, it's possible that he carved Garfield before Lincoln. Like McKinley, Garfield had been assassinated during Brice's lifetime.

Lincoln stands only a few yards from the statue of McKinley, directly in front of Noah Baughman's house. President Lincoln was killed when Noah was fifteen years old, so it's possible that Noah asked Brice to carve Lincoln, or maybe Brice chose to carve Lincoln as a gift to his father.

HIGHLIGHTS OF LINCOLN'S LIFE

Abe Lincoln was born in Kentucky in 1809. A few years later he moved with his parents to Indiana. Altogether he obtained less than a year of formal education. He later studied law and served briefly in the Illinois State Militia as a private and a captain.

Lincoln served in the U.S. House of Representatives and eventually was elected to the presidency. He was devoted to the preservation of the Union and led the nation during its long and bloody Civil War. In 1863 he issued his Emancipation Proclamation which declared freedom for slaves.

Lincoln was re-elected in the election of 1864. In his inaugural address he outlined a program designed to reunite the North and South after the war was over. On April 14, 1865, only five days after Lee's surrender, President Lincoln was killed by an assassin while enjoying a play in Washington. He was the first U. S. president to be assassinated.

Above: President Lincoln.

Opposite: An early photo of Brice's statue of Lincoln standing behind the white picket fence in front of Noah Baughman's house.
(Photo Courtesy of Lester Baughman)

Inscription on the Statue
(shown exactly as carved)

Front

LINCOLN

IN
HONOR. G.A.R.
COSHOCTON

Right: Brice putting some of the final details on the Lincoln statue in the quarry. He used a large wooden mallet to strike his chisels.
(Photo courtesy of Ray Murray)

Below: One of the strange scenes at Baughman Park: Abraham Lincoln stands proudly in front of a dilapidated house.
(A. Keirns photo '97)

Above & Left: Views of the Lincoln statue as it appears today.
(A. Keirns photos '00)

Honest Abe Visited Frazeysburg

It's not widely known, but Abraham Lincoln and his wife once visited the village of Frazeysburg. It happened in 1860 when President-elect Lincoln was traveling between Columbus and the nation's capitol. According to a *Zanesville Courier* report of the time:

"A subscriber writes from Frazeysburg, in this county, that the president and his suite passed through their village about 10 o'clock on Thursday morning, on a special train over the Steubenville and Indiana Railroad. Notwithstanding the pouring rain, a very large number of citizens of all parties were present to welcome him. Mr. Lincoln appeared on the platform and spoke a few words, when the crowd gave three cheers for Lincoln and the Union. The people were all delighted with the honest looking face of the president elect."

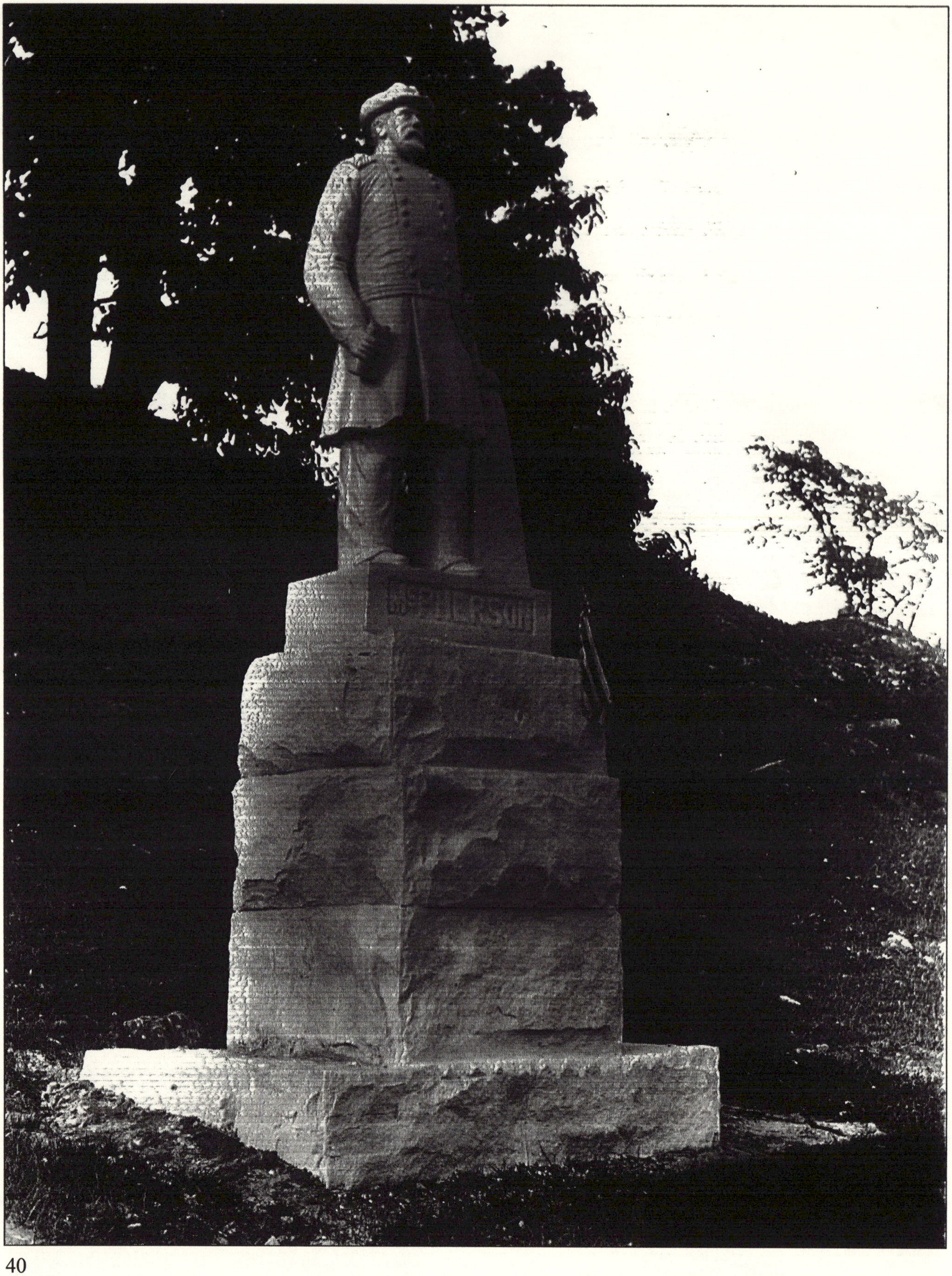

JAMES B. MCPHERSON

MAJOR GENERAL, UNION ARMY
KILLED IN BATTLE, 1864

General James Birdseye McPherson was a distinguished military leader during America's Civil War. As mentioned earlier, Brice may have chosen to place McPherson in the same row of statues as Presidents McKinley, Lincoln and Garfield because, like them, he was killed while in service to his country. McPherson was also a fellow Ohioan and greatly respected by two of Brice's other subjects: Ulysses S. Grant and William T. Sherman.

Brice's statue of McPherson shows him in full uniform complete with sword, binoculars and hat. The only other statue in Baughman Park wearing a hat is the Doughboy.

HIGHLIGHTS OF MCPHERSON'S LIFE

James B. McPherson was born in Clyde, Ohio, in 1828. He secured an appointment to West Point where he graduated first in his class. He served in various positions in the Union Army and eventually became head of the Army of the Tennessee.

During the Battle of Atlanta, General Mcpherson came upon a group of Confederate skirmishers and was mortally wounded. He was the highest ranking Union officer to be killed in battle during the Civil War. His body is buried in the McPherson Cemetery in Clyde, Ohio.

Generals Grant and Sherman both took McPherson's death very personally. "General McPherson fell booted and spurred as the gallant and heroic gentleman should wish," lamented Sherman.

In a poignant letter to McPherson's aged grandmother, Grant wrote: "Your bereavement is great, but cannot exceed mine."

DEDICATION

On September 19, 1914, the statues of General McPherson and President Garfield were dedicated. McPherson was dedicated to the Frazeysburg G.A.R., and Garfield was dedicated to the G.A.R. of

Above: Major General McPherson.

Opposite: Early photo of McPherson statue before the G. A. R. inscription was added to the front.
(Photo Courtesy of Ray Murray)

Inscription on the Statue
(shown exactly as carved)

Front

MCPHERSON

IN HONOR. G.A.R.

FRAZEYSBURG

Side

CAPTIAN
JOHN A. EVANS
27 OHIO

Above: McPherson statue today.

Top Right: McPherson statue while still in the quarry. The man in the photo is John A. Evans who served under McPherson in the Civil War.
(Photo Courtesy of Ray Murray)

Opposite: Brice puts the finishing touches on McPherson.
(Photo Courtesy of Lester Baughman)

Columbus. The event was "largely attended," according to a newspaper report in the *Zanesville Signal*.

In attendance were the G. A. R. post of Frazeysburg, the Newark Old Guards and the Old Guard Drum Corps of Columbus. The report also mentions a "Black Run Memorial Society."

One of the speakers at the event was Capt. John A. Evans whose name is now inscribed for eternity on the side of the McPherson statue. The Newark D. A. R. (Daughters of the American Revolution) were also in attendance and presented a flag which was run up a flag pole.

The newspaper reported ended by saying: "Mr. Baughman, who donated the park and statues, was unable to attend the dedication as he was called away on professional business, being an undertaker."

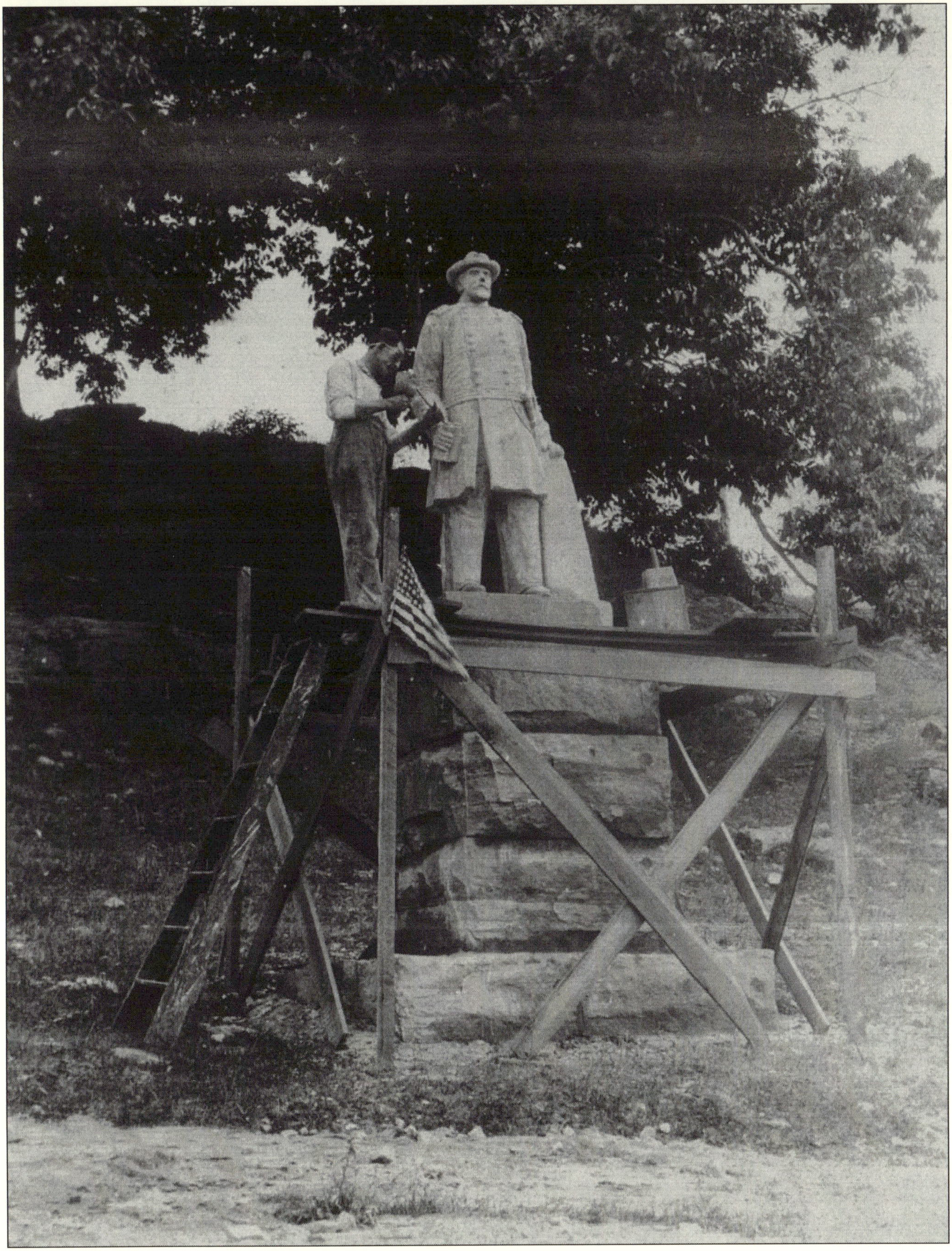

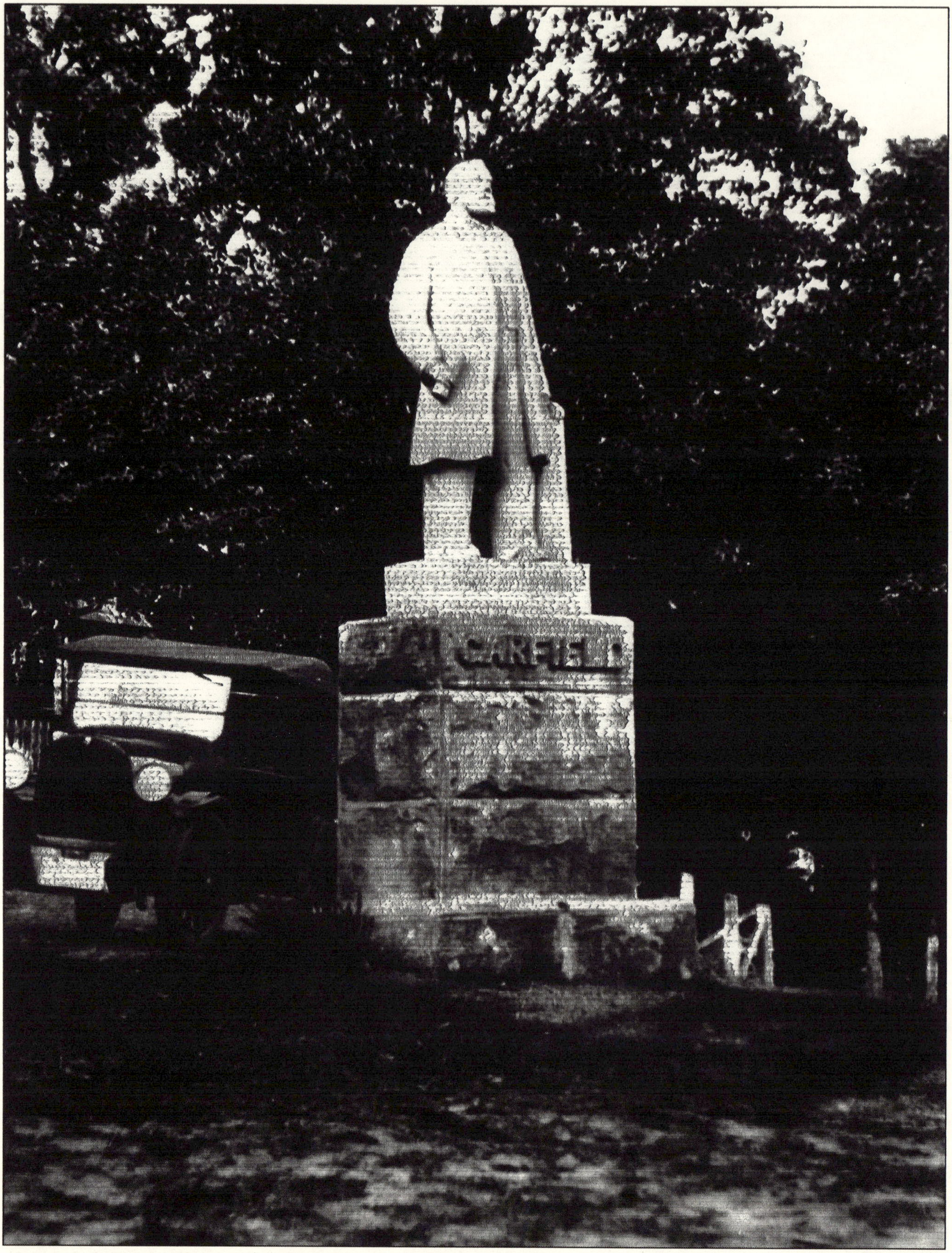
GARFIELD

James A. Garfield

Twentieth President
1881

Brice Baughman must have had a great respect for James A. Garfield. Of all the statues he created, it was Garfield that Brice chose to put in his own front yard. Brice was seven years old when President Garfield was shot and killed. This incident no doubt left a lasting impression on young Brice.

Garfield also had a local connection. In the Spring of 1851, Garfield taught school for three months in Muskingum County. The little log school house was located in Harrison Township, southeast of Zanesville.

Like the other statues in Baughman Park, Garfield faces south, looking out over the valley below. The Garfield statue is unique in that it sits in the middle of a circular driveway.

Highlights of Garfield's Life

James A. Garfield was born in Cuyahoga County, Ohio in 1831. Known as the last of the "log cabin presidents," Garfield surmounted poverty and earned money for college by driving canal boat teams.

He eventually became a classics professor and president of a college. Later he was elected to the Ohio Senate. He also served in the military, successfully leading a brigade at Middle Creek, Kentucky, against Confederate troops. He achieved the ranks of brigadier general and major general of volunteers. At President Lincoln's urging, Garfield resigned his commission and was elected to Congress.

After serving several years in Congress, Garfield ran for President and was elected in 1880. As President, he began to fight vigorously against political patronage and corruption. Unfortunately, only six months after taking office, Garfield was shot twice in the back by an embittered attorney in Washington. Several medical procedures were performed on the President, but all proved unsuccessful. After lying wounded in the White House for several weeks, he was taken to the New Jersey seaside where his condition seemed to improve slightly. Then, less than two weeks later, on September 19, 1881, President Garfield died of his wounds.

-Above: President Garfield.

Opposite: An early photo of Garfield statue in front of Brice's house.
(Photo Courtesy of Bill Weaver)

Inscription on the Statue
(shown exactly as carved)

Front

GARFIELD

Side

DEDICATED
SEPt. 19. 1914
IN HONOR
G. A. R.
COLUMBUS

MANY ATTENDED STATUE DEDICATION

Largely attended was the dedication Saturday of Memorial park on the Brice Baughman farm at Black Run and the statues of President Garfield and Gen. J. B. McPherson, chiseled by Mr. Baughman. The Black Run Memorial society was assisted in the dedication by the G. A. R. post of Fraseyburg, the Newark Old Guards and the Old Guard drum corps of Columbus.

The speakers in the morning were Capt. J. A. Evans, Fraseyburg; H. W. Kunts, Zanesville, and Rev. R. L. Kilpatrick of Perryton. The chairman was J. G. Frampton of Perryton. In the afternoon addresses were made by Oscar W. Sheppard of West Alexandria, and Judge W. A. Irwin, of Newark.

The Newark D. A. R. presented a flag, which was run up on a flag pole. The Newark Old Guards fired a salute and the Columbus drum corps played martial airs.

Mr. Baughman, who has donated the park and statues, was unable to attend the dedication as he was called away on professional business, being an undertaker.

-*Above:* Newspaper report from the Zanesville Signal, Sept. 21, 1914.

Top Right: In this 1880 campaign poster, Garfield "cuts a swath" to the White House.

A Promising Leader

Of all the presidential assassinations, the death of Garfield was, in some ways, the most cruel. After being shot, he laid in bed for weeks, slowly dying from his wounds. But perhaps the cruelest blow was that Garfield was a promising leader, poised to accomplish much for the country, yet he was cut down after barely six months in office.

Hidden Bullet

When President Garfield was shot, he underwent numerous medical treatments, but it was clear that he was losing the battle. The problem was a bullet lodged in Garfield's back that couldn't be located. (Unfortunately this was fourteen years before the discovery of x-rays.)

One of the most unusual attempts to save the President came from Alexander Graham Bell, renowned inventor of the telephone.

Bell came to the White House where Garfield lay wounded and tried to locate the bullet with his newly invented "induction balance electrical device." But despite Bell's best efforts, his device was unsuccessful in locating the hidden bullet. President Garfield died a few weeks later.

Above: The Garfield statue stands beneath a huge pine tree, his head nearly obscured by its branches.
(A. Keirns photo '98)

Left: Close-up of Garfield statue.
(A. Keirns photo '00)

47

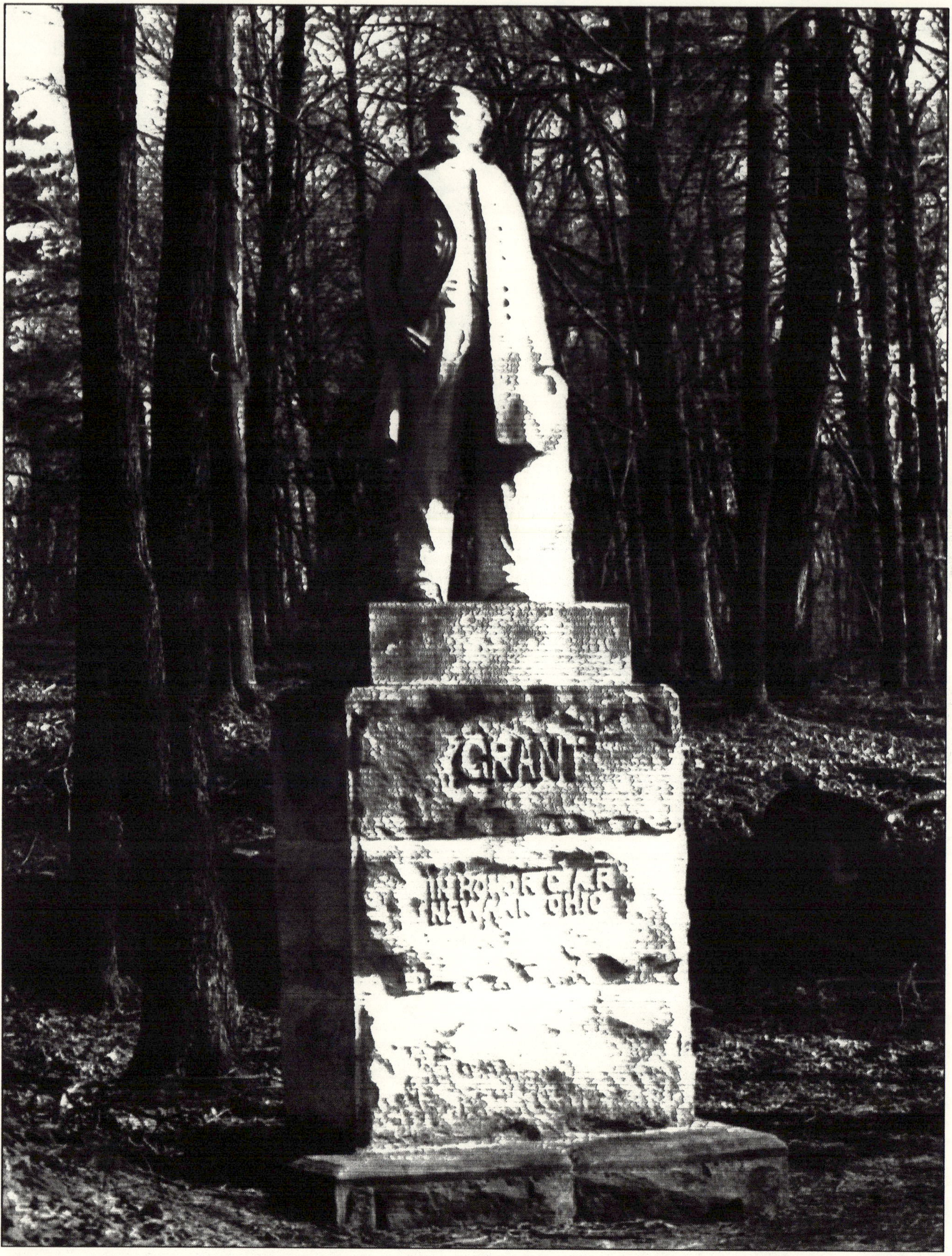
GRANT

ULYSSES S. GRANT

GENERAL OF THE ARMY, 1866
EIGHTEENTH PRESIDENT, 1869-1877

The statue of Ulysses S. Grant in Baughman Park is one of Brice Baughman's finest works. Grant stands about half way up the hill in an area often referred to as the amphitheater. This is perhaps Brice's most natural-looking sculpture. Grant's head is slightly turned, with eyes raised, gazing far off into the distance. As he looks toward the south, he seems to be in deep thought, as if contemplating the devastation he witnessed during the Civil War.

Brice was even creative in the way he carved the word "Grant" into the front of the statue. Unlike his other statues which have flat block lettering, Brice sculpted Grant's name with an artistic wood-like effect.

PRESIDENT OR GENERAL?

It's interesting that Brice chose to portray Grant in military uniform. This leaves little doubt that the statue is intended to represent Grant the General, not Grant the President. None of the other Presidents on Baughman hill are shown in uniform, even though they all had served as military officers (with the exception of Harding).

Ulysses S. Grant was a brilliant military strategist but a rather dismal president. Brice apparently chose to depict Grant as he was in his finest hour – the preeminent Union hero of the Civil War.

HIGHLIGHTS OF GRANT'S LIFE

Hiram Ulysses Grant was born in Point Pleasant, Ohio, in 1822. He entered the United States Military Academy in 1839 but had no real plans for a military career. Due to a clerical error, he was registered as Ulysses Simpson Grant, a name he chose to keep.

Grant served in the Mexican War (1846-48) and fought with distinction, emerging as a first lieutenant. He later served other tours of duty in New York, Detroit and even California. After a dispute with his commanding officer, Grant resigned from military service in 1854.

Above: General Grant.

Opposite: The Grant statue as it appears today.
(A. Keirns photo)

Inscription on the Statue
(shown exactly as carved)

<u>Front</u>

GRANT

IN HONOR G.A.R.
NEWARK OHIO

<u>Side</u>

USA

An Invitation Declined

After his victories in the Civil War, U. S. Grant was treated like a celebrity in the North. He was mobbed by crowds of well-wishers wherever he went.

In April of 1865, President Lincoln invited Grant and his wife to attend a play with the Lincolns at Ford's Theater in Washington. Grant declined the invitation.

Little did Grant know that this night at Ford's Theater would witness one of the most tragic events in American history. A gunman entered the President's box and shot President Lincoln. The President died a few hours later.

If Grant had attended the play with the Lincolns in their private box that night, he might very well have been assassinated along with the President. Or, perhaps he may have prevented it.

Right: Viewed from the driveway below, Grant creates a striking image among the trees.
(A. Keirns photo '97)

Above: Brice (in white) Gov. Willis, and others in front of Grant statue.
(Photo courtesy of Ray Murray)

When the Civil War broke out, Grant found a position commanding a militia outfit from Illinois. He quickly rose through the ranks and eventually took command of all Union Forces. He became well-known as a great strategist and natural military leader. His coordinated offensive against the Confederacy resulted in the end of the war in 1865.

After the war Grant remained at the head of the Army and received the title of General of the Army. He had become a national figure and a likely candidate for the presidency. In 1868 he won the Republican nomination and the election. He began his first term as President in 1869.

Grant was a superb General but not so well-suited to politics. He was honest and naive, attributes that others took advantage of. Even though his presidency was plagued by scandal, Grant was reelected for a second term in 1872.

After his presidency, Grant and his wife toured the world for two years. Later, in 1880, he once again sought the Republican Presidential nomination but lost to James A. Garfield.

Grant's life went downhill in his later years. Failed business ventures, lack of money and throat cancer took their toll on the aged veteran. At the end of his life he frantically wrote his memoirs in hopes they would bring some income to his family. In 1885, a few days after he finished writing, he died. Grant's memoirs eventually earned his heirs nearly half a million dollars in royalties.

Three in a Row

It's well-known that the State of Ohio has produced several of our nation's Presidents. In the late 1800's there were actually three Presidents in a row from Ohio. Ulysses S. Grant was the first, followed by Rutherford B. Hayes and James A. Garfield, all Republicans.

Left: Brice's artistic talent is beautifully displayed in the Grant statue.
(A. Keirns photo '00)

Above: Details of Grant statue.
(A. Keirns photos '01)

51

52

GEORGE WASHINGTON

FIRST PRESIDENT
1789-1797

When Brice placed George Washington's statue at the top of Baughman's hill, it must have been an impressive sight. The hill wasn't covered with trees and brush as it is today. Washington stood alone on the summit with an unobstructed view for miles in every direction. To the folks down below in Black Run, Washington's gleaming white figure looked like a sentinel standing guard over the valley.

MASONIC INFLUENCE

Brice was a member of the Free and Accepted Masons, a fraternal organization also known as the Freemasons or Masons. The Masons are the oldest secret society in the world. It is thought that Freemasonry evolved from the medieval guilds of stonemasons – a connection certainly not lost on Brice Baughman.

George Washington was one of America's first Masons, as were most of the signers of the Declaration of Independence. Freemasonry has been a powerful force in politics for hundreds of years. There are a variety of mysterious symbols associated with the Masons, even U. S. Currency contains Masonic symbols. It's no coincidence that our one dollar bill (with Washington on the front) shows a pyramid on the back with a missing capstone and "all-seeing eye," both long-standing Masonic symbols.

Brice carved several Masonic symbols into Washington's statue. What's even more unique about the statue however, is that Washington is shown wearing a Masonic apron. This may be one of the only statues in existence showing Washington in Masonic regalia.

AN ANACHRONISM

Probably the oddest thing about the Washington statue is something often overlooked by visitors – his pants. During Washington's time, gentlemen wore knee-breeches. These were short, tight-fitting pants that ended just below the knee. Knee-breeches were usually accompanied by

Above: President Washington.

Opposite: An early photo of the Washington statue.
(Photo Courtesy of Ray Murray)

Inscription on the Statue
(shown exactly as carved)

<u>**Front**</u>

G. WASHINGTON

<u>**Side**</u>

IN HONOR
F. AND. A. M
OF OHIO

F.M. FLEMING
A.H. THOMSON
F.M. RANSBOTOM
COMMITTEE

Above: This statue, located in the State Capitol Building in Richmond, Virginia, shows a typical depiction of Washington in his knee-breeches.

Right: Brice's statue of Washington as it appears today, standing in the edge of a woods.
(A. Keirns photo '98)

high silk stockings or tall boots. Brice's statue depicts Washington in full-length pants, a modern garment. Brice knew the long pants were not historically correct, but he feared that carving Washington in knee-breeches would make the legs too thin to support the weight of the statue.

Brice ran into a similar problem when he carved the Doughboy. This time his solution was to carve a massive support into the statue just behind the legs.

HIGHLIGHTS OF WASHINGTON'S LIFE

George Washington was born in Virginia in 1732. He was commissioned as a lieutenant colonel in 1754 and fought the first skirmishes of

Left: Washington is one of Brice's most highly-detailed works.
(A. Keirns photo '00)

Above: Several cryptic Freemasonry symbols adorn Washington's statue.
(A. Keirns photo '97)

what would become the French and Indian War. In 1775 he was elected Commander in Chief of the Continental Army. For six grueling years he led the fight against the British. Finally, in 1781 he helped force the surrender of Cornwallis at Yorktown.

When the new Constitution was ratified, the Electoral College unanimously elected Washington as our nation's first President. He served as President for two terms, then retired to Mount Vernon where he died of a throat infection in 1799.

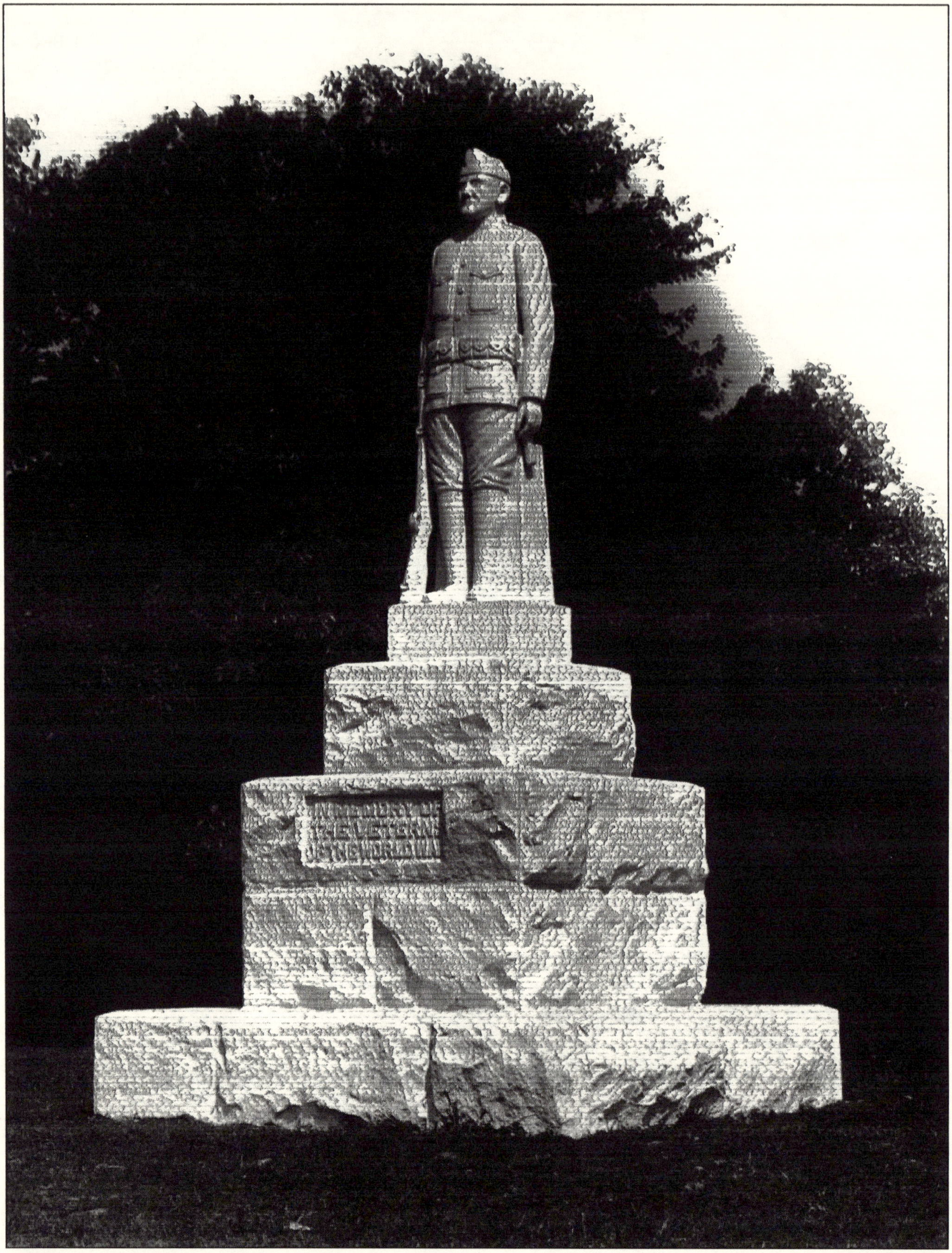

The Doughboy

World War I Soldier
1917-1918

Of all the statues Brice Baughman carved, the Doughboy was said to be his favorite. For this statue he chose not to portray a high-ranking officer or well-known hero. Instead, he honored all the veterans of World War I by depicting an ordinary, nameless soldier – or perhaps the "unknown soldier." This is the only statue Brice carved that didn't represent a particular individual.

Brice's Doughboy stands at attention, tall and rigid with rifle and bayonet close at hand. His uniform is meticulously detailed with buttoned pockets, ammo belt and leggings.

Originally there were two real machine guns mounted on the Doughboy statue but they were stolen. There was also a World War I howitzer (cannon) displayed in front of the statue. Brice may have donated it to a scrap metal drive during World War II along with two Civil War cannons that were displayed in the park.

Lightning Strikes

Lightning once struck the Doughboy statue, splitting the head and damaging other areas of the figure. Brice repaired (or replaced?) the head and patched the other damaged parts. Some of these patches are still visible, especially in the area of the rifle.

The World War I Soldier

"Doughboy" was a slang term often applied to infantrymen, especially during WWI. The term is thought to have originated from the small boiled dumplings or doughnuts that were a staple of military diet at the time.

Although WWI began in 1914, the United States didn't officially get involved until 1917. When President Woodrow Wilson called for a declaration of war against Germany, the U. S. Army had a grand total of 200,000 men, 55 rickety planes and 130 pilots. Equipment was so scarce that the British and French had to sell American troops most of their artil-

---

Inscription on the Statue
(shown exactly as carved)

Front

MUSKINGUM COUNTY

IN MEMORY OF
THE VETERNS
OF THE WORLD WAR

Back

DEDICATED BY
ZANESVILLE
POST NO. 29
AMERICAN
LEGION.
AUG. 28 1921

Opposite: An early photo of the Doughboy statue. Notice that "Muskingum County," has not yet been carved into the top block.

(Photo Courtesy of Ray Murray)

BAUGHMAN PARK SERVICE DREW MONSTER CROWD

Thousands of visitors were in attendance at the unveiling and dedication of the "Doughboy" monument in Baughman park Sunday afternoon. The crowd was estimated at seven thousand and the automobiles in the park at the time of the ceremony numbered close to two thousand. The local American Legion chapter attended the service in a body and in addition to these many other Zanesville people motored to the beautiful park for the ceremony.

The services opened with a selection by the Mark American (old Seventh) band. Following this, Captain John Evans of Frazeysburg, presented the monument and in appropriate words told of the significance of the erection of such a monument.

The monument was unveiled by Mrs. Anna Daniels, president of the Woman's Auxiliary of Zanesville. During the unveiling and immediately following the Mark American band played several appropriate selections.

The principal address of the afternoon was made by Col. John R. McQuigg of Cleveland, head of the American Legion of Ohio. Colonel McQuigg in speaking of the affair said that the unveiling Sunday was one of the finest services he had ever witnessed. His speech was in keeping with the occasion and was greeted with applause at its conclusion.

The program closed with a tribute in rhyme to Brice Baughman who owns Baughman park, and who carved the statue of the doughboy from rock.

Colonel McQuigg said during the course of his address, that the Zanesville post of the American Legion was one of the livest organizations in the state and that more progress had been made by the local post than any other post in the Ohio division. "I'm certainly well pleased with the spirit shown by Legion members in Zanesville," said Colonel McQuigg.

Exceptional credit is given to the 20 boys of Troop 15 of Grace M. E. church, who ably handled the traffic situation in the park. Although the number of automobiles in the park exceeded any previous record, the boys succeeded in keeping the cars from becoming congested. Automobile owners were loud in their praise of the work of the troop.

Above: The Doughboy was dedicated on Aug. 28, 1921, as reported in this news item from the following day.

---

lery, tanks, and ammunition.

The American people quickly rallied to the cause however, and soon were producing tons of equipment and food for the men fighting overseas. As the men were called into service, the women they left behind took over their jobs. It was a time of great patriotism.

The entire conflict lasted a little over four years. A total of nine million soldiers died on both sides and another eighteen million were wounded. Ten million civilians also died. America lost 116,000 men, more than half of which died from disease.

DEDICATION

The dedication of the Doughboy statue is well-documented. It took place on Sunday, Aug. 28, 1921. The statue was dedicated by the Zanesville American Legion. Many veterans participated, including veterans of the Civil War and Spanish-American War.

Capt. John A. Evans of Frazeysburg presented the statue and gave a brief speech. This was the same Capt. Evans that spoke at the dedication of the McPherson and Garfield statues seven years earlier. The number of people attending the Doughboy dedication was estimated at 7,000 along with more than 2000 automobiles.

Above: Originally placed in a clearing, the Doughboy is now shrouded by huge pine trees.
(A. Keirns photo '98)

Top Center: A damaged, but wonderful, panoramic photograph taken during the dedication of the Doughboy. Brice is standing in the top row, left of the statue with his arms crossed.
(Photo courtesy of Ray Murray)

Lower Left: A detail from the above panoramic photo.

Above: One of the two WWI machine guns that were mounted on the Doughboy statue.
(Photo Courtesy of Curtis "Bud" Abbott)

59

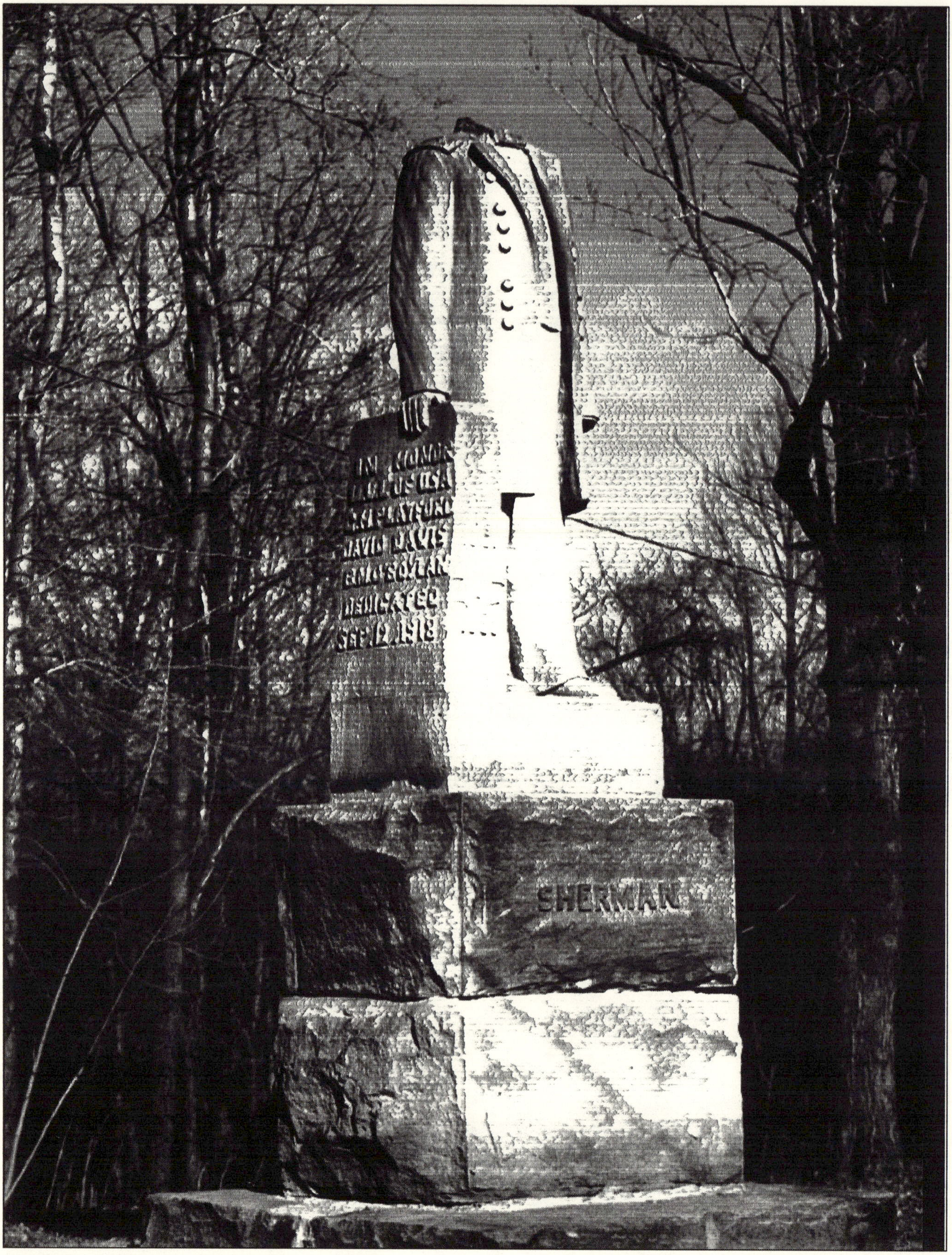
SHERMAN

WILLIAM T. SHERMAN

GENERAL OF THE ARMY, 1869
RETIRED 1884

*L*ike the other two Civil War generals Brice sculpted, William T. Sherman was an Ohioan. Brice seemed to have a deep interest in the Civil War. He lived during a time when the war was still a common topic of conversation. Many veterans of the war were still living and huge reunions were often held. Even small communities such as the nearby village of Toboso hosted reunions for the veterans. In 1900 the Toboso reunion attracted an estimated six thousand people.

Brice was in his late teens when Sherman died, so he had no doubt heard many stories about Sherman's military achievements. Among the Union generals, Sherman was second in importance only to Grant. When Grant became President in 1869, Sherman took over his position as commander of the U. S. Army.

VANDALS ON THE HILL

In 1968 vandals broke off the heads of two statues in Baughman Park: Roosevelt and Sherman. Sherman's left hand is also missing. Roosevelt's head was eventually returned and reattached, but Sherman's head has yet to be located. Hopefully, his head and hand will someday be found and returned to the park where they can be reattached.

HIGHLIGHTS OF SHERMAN'S LIFE

William Tecumseh Sherman was born in Lancaster, Ohio, in 1820. He graduated from West Point in 1840 and served in the Mexican War. In 1853 he resigned from the army to pursue careers in banking and law.

At the start of the Civil War, Sherman rejoined the army as a colonel. He eventually rose to the rank of brigadier general of volunteers and then major general. After the battle of Vicksburg in 1863, he was promoted to brigadier general in the Regular Army and placed in command of the Army of the Tennessee, a command later held by General McPherson.

Sherman is perhaps best remembered for his famous (or infamous)

Above: General Sherman.

Opposite: The Sherman statue as it appears today.
(A. Keirns photo)

Inscription on the Statue
(shown exactly as carved)

<u>Front</u>

SHERMAN

<u>Side</u>

IN HONOR
U.V.L. OF USA
G.H. PLAYFORD
DAVID DAVIS
B.M. O' BOYLAN
DEDICATED
SEP. 12. 1918

61

Above: Detail of Sherman statue.
(A. Keirns photo '01)

Right: Brice puts the finishing touches on the Sherman statue while two ladies look on, ca. 1918.
(Photo courtesy of Ray Murray)

burning of Atlanta and subsequent "march to the sea." He reasoned that civilian morale and economic resources were just as important targets as the enemy's armies. His troops cut a wide swath of devastation across the south, eventually leading to the surrender of the last major Confederate army in the east.

In 1869 Sherman succeeded Grant as commander of the Army and concentrated on controlling the Plains Indians. In 1884 he retired from military service. Although offered opportunities in politics, he declined, and was quoted as saying: "I will not accept if nominated and will not serve if elected."

Sherman published his memoirs in 1875 and, like Grant's, they are considered classics of military literature. Sherman died in New York City in the winter of 1891.

Above: Picture of the Sherman statue from the souvenir booklet printed for the park dedication in 1931.

Left: Detail of Sherman uniform.
(A. Keirns photo '00)

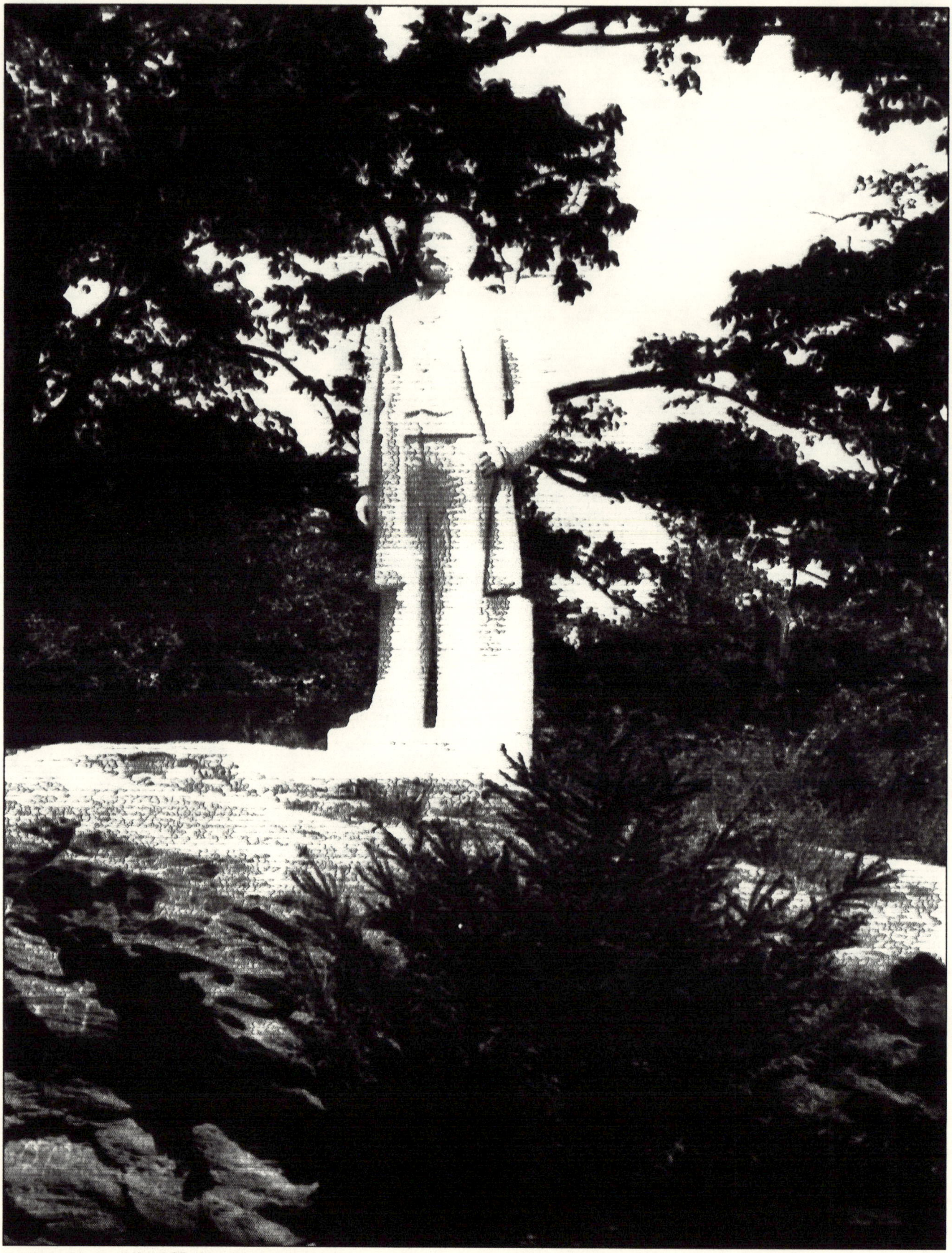

THEODORE ROOSEVELT

TWENTY-SIXTH PRESIDENT
1901-1909

The statue of Theodore Roosevelt occupies a unique setting in Baughman Park. Unlike the other statues, Roosevelt is mounted directly on a natural rock formation. He stands high on a sandstone ledge not far from the quarry where he originated.

Roosevelt's statue is highly detailed and includes the President's distinctive wire rim spectacles and even his watch chain. The smooth white statue sitting atop the dark sandstone makes a striking combination.

As mentioned earlier, Roosevelt's head was broken off and stolen in 1968 along with Sherman's head. The heads were apparently taken as part of a college prank. Roosevelt's head was later located and returned to Ray Murray, the park's owner at the time. Mr. Murray skillfully reattached the head and today the break is barely discernible. Hopefully the same will happen with the Sherman statue some day.

HIGHLIGHTS OF ROOSEVELT'S LIFE

Theodore "Teddy" Roosevelt was born in lower Manhattan in 1858. Unlike some of the other Presidents, Roosevelt was born into a wealthy family. He too had his struggles, however. He was asthmatic in childhood, nearsighted and frail. He was determined to build his body and participated in sports, exercise and outdoor activities. He became a lifelong champion of physical fitness.

He graduated from Harvard University in 1880 where he began writing his first book on naval history. It would be the first of 40 books and many articles he would write on history, politics and adventure.

Roosevelt began his political career in 1882 when he won a seat in the State Legislature. In 1884 his wife and mother died on the same day. Roosevelt was grief-stricken and soon headed out to the Badlands of the Dakota Territory where had visited the previous year and had invested in a cattle ranch. For several years he lived the life of the cowboy.

He went on to hold other offices such as president of the New York

Above: President Roosevelt.

Opposite: An early photo of the Roosevelt statue.
(Courtesy of Curtis "Bud" Abbott)

Inscription on the Statue
(shown exactly as carved)

Front

ROOSEVELT

Back

DEDICATED BY
NEWARK NO. 77
AUXILIARY AND
SONS OF
VETERANS
JUNE 27. 1926
IDA BILLMAN
LOU ADKINS
CORA L. FLYNN
C.S. OSBURN

Above: Roosevelt statue today.
(A. Keirns photos '01)

Top Right: Brice Baughman with his monument to Roosevelt, ca. 1950.
(Photo courtesy of Lester Baughman)

City Board of Police Commissioners and Assistant Secretary of the Navy. When the Spanish-American War broke out in 1898, Roosevelt accepted the position of lieutenant-colonel in a national volunteer cavalry regiment called the "Rough Riders." He displayed bravery in action in Cuba, was promoted to colonel and came home a hero.

After the war, Roosevelt was elected Governor of New York and then Vice President to William McKinley. After only six months as Vice President, Roosevelt inherited the presidency when McKinley was assassinated in 1901.

Roosevelt was a powerful and energetic President. He inaugurated a Department of Commerce and Labor, helped build some of America's largest dams, and set up a Forest Service. He was also instrumental in building the Panama Canal and strengthening the U. S. Navy. He was

ROOSEVELT MONUMENT AT BAUGHMAN PARK IS UNVEILED BY VETERANS

The Sons of Veterans unveiled the Roosevelt statue which is the handiwork of Bryce Baughman, at his home, Baughman Park, near Black Run yesterday.

The unveiling was under the auspices of the Newark Sons of Veterans. A. E. Deems, national patriotic instructor of the Sons of Veterans of Los Angeles; Mrs. Mamie Deems, national president of the Ladies' Auxiliary, and Mrs. Carrie E. Williams, national vice president delivered the addresses.

The event was attended by five thousand people.

Above: News item tells of Roosevelt statue dedication on June 27, 1926, an event attended by 5,000 people.

Above: Detail of Doris & Geraldene Cameron from photograph at left.

Left: Roosevelt statue in the quarry ca. 1925-26. Long mast with ropes and pulleys is part of the derrick used to lift and maneuver the statues.

(Courtesy of Ray Murray)

easily elected for a second term but declined to run for a third.

Later, Roosevelt ran again for President but was defeated by Woodrow Wilson. During Roosevelt's campaign, he was shot in the chest by an assassin but survived. During his later years, he continued to write and make frequent speeches. He died in 1919 of an heart embolism.

67

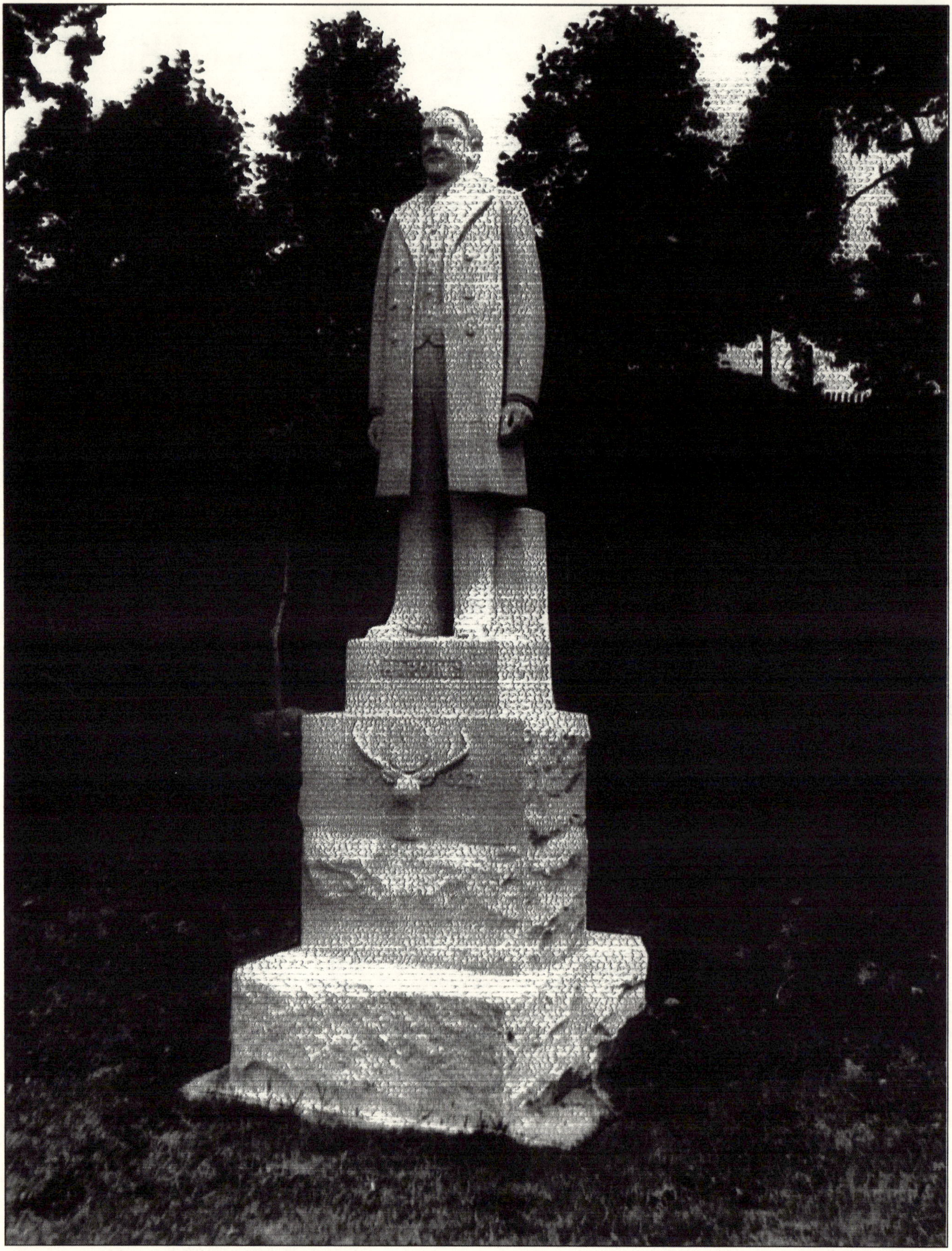

WARREN G. HARDING

TWENTY-NINTH PRESIDENT
1921-1923

Warren G. Harding is the last statue Brice Baughman carved. He had plans to carve other statues, including Ohio Governor, Vic Donahey, and General Douglas MacArthur. Brice was 53 years old when the Harding statue was dedicated. A case of scarlet fever left his throat in such a sensitive condition that stone dust caused irritation. Brice reluctantly had to suspend his carving activity. He hoped to take up carving again after WWII, but due to his failing health, was unable to carry out his plans to carve more statues.

The Harding statue stands along the road leading into the park from State Route 586. It's an impressive statue, tall and stately. On the base, Brice carved an elk head in honor of the Benevolent and Protective Order of Elks (B. P. O. E.) of which Brice and President Harding were members. Between the antlers of the elk is a clock face which seems to be set at the eleventh hour.

Above: President Harding.
Opposite: An early photo of the Harding statue.
(Courtesy of Curtis "Bud" Abbott)

HIGHLIGHTS OF HARDING'S LIFE

Warren Gamaliel Harding was born on a farm at Corsica, in north-central Ohio in 1865. He earned a B.S. degree from Ohio Central College in 1882. After college he held several jobs including teaching and insurance sales. He became a newspaper reporter and eventually publisher of the Marion Star newspaper.

Harding entered politics as a county auditor and later became State Senator and Lieutenant Governor. He then served in the U. S. Senate and was elected President in the election of 1920.

During his presidency, Harding tried to carry out his promise of "Less government in business and more business in government." He won accolades from the public for his diplomatic achievements and for reviving prosperity. But behind the scenes, some of his friends were using their official positions for their personal gain. Harding was strongly effected by the rumors of this unethical activity and worried about the scandal that might develop. He wouldn't live long enough to find out.

Inscription on the Statue
(shown exactly as carved)

Front

HARDING

B.P. O.E.

R.W. SMITH   U.R. COOPER
H.D. HALE   J.C. BROWN

Back

DEDICATED
BY NEWARK
LODGE OF
ELKS 391
B.P.O.E.
JUNE 12
1927

Above: Statues of Harding and Roosevelt in the quarry, suggesting that Brice may have worked on more than one statue at a time. Notice the derrick with its vertical mast and cranking wheel or windlass at the bottom. The movable arm of the derrick is angled out toward Roosevelt and is partially hidden by the trees.
(Photo courtesy of Ray Murray)

Below: Back of Harding statue.
(A. Keirns photo '01)

While traveling in the West in 1923, Harding received details of the magnitude of the corruption that had infected his administration. He became ill in Alaska and died in San Francisco on the return trip. He was 58 years old.

TEN THOUSAND ATTEND DEDICATION

The statue of Harding was dedicated on Sunday, June 12, 1927. By this time, Baughman Memorial Park had become well-known and Brice's work was widely admired. The crowds grew larger at each dedication, swelling to over 10,000 at the Harding event. The number of automobiles at the park that day numbered 3,640. "The roads between Zanesville and Frazeysburg were lined with automobiles to and from the park." reported a Zanesville newspaper.

A news item in the *Dresden Transcript,* announcing plans for dedication of the Harding statue, referred to Brice as the "genius known as the farmer-undertaker sculptor." And that, he was.

THOUSANDS VISIT BAUGHMAN PARK FOR DEDICATION

It was estimated that more than ten thousand people from throughout Ohio attended the unveiling and dedication of the late President Warren G. Harding statue at Baughman Memorial park, near Black Run, Sunday afternoon.

A number from Zanesville attended the affair and the roads between Zanesville and Frazeysburg were lined with automobiles to and from the park. Many made it an all day affair, and carried well filled baskets to the park where they enjoyed a picnic dinner.

The Harding statue is the work of Brice Baughman, farmer-sculptor, who is proprietor of the park, and the likeness of the late president was carved from native rock. The exercises were under the auspices of the Newark lodge of Elks, and a fine program followed the ceremonies. Judge Charles L. Justice of Marion, delivered the dedicatory address. President Harding was an honorary life member of the Marion lodge of Elks.

Above: News item about the Harding dedication *(Zanesville Signal).*

Left and Bottom Left: The Harding statue as it appears today.
(A. Keirns photos '01)

Harding Was Wilson

The statue of Harding started out to be President Wilson.

In the early 1920's Brice had begun to rough-out a statue of Woodrow Wilson (President from 1913 to 1921). Wilson was still living at the time.

Someone suggested to Brice that it was premature to hew the statue of a living man. About the same time, President Harding unexpectedly died in office.

When Harding died in 1923, Brice gradually transformed the Wilson statue into the likeness of his successor in the White House, Warren G. Harding.

The Harding statue was dedicated in 1927 which means it was at least 4 years between the time Brice started carving and the time the statue was dedicated.

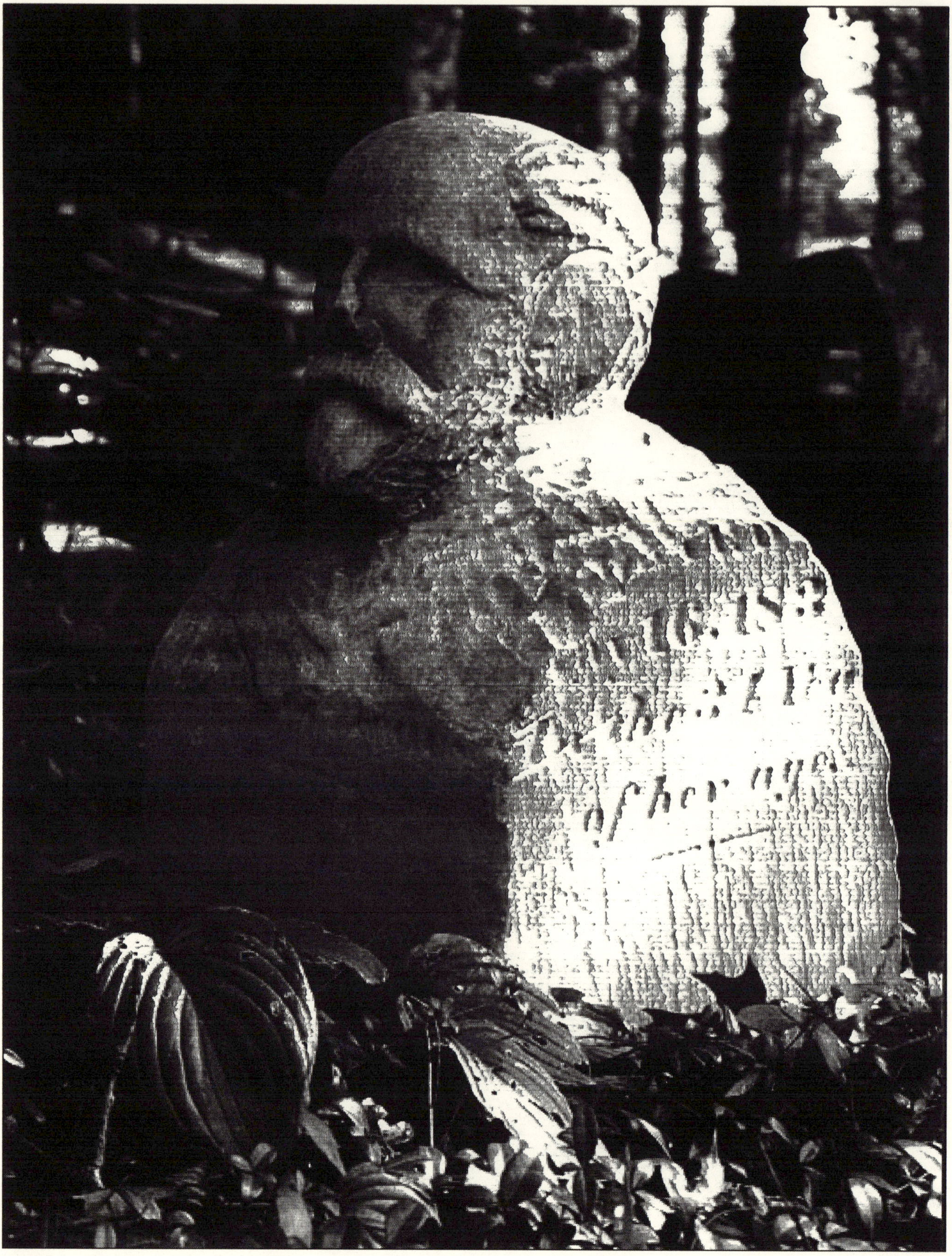
of her age

CHAPTER FIVE

ODDS & ENDS AROUND THE PARK

Several items in Baughman Park are not easily categorized and so are grouped together here as odds & ends. These works include: a marble bust of William Shakespeare; cannon mounts; a stone watering trough; flower vases; inscribed wall and even a "ghost rock."

WILLIAM SHAKESPEARE

One of the most unusual sculptures Brice carved was a marble bust of the English playwright, William Shakespeare. Not only is the subject of this sculpture an odd choice for Brice, it was the only carving he ever did in something other than sandstone.

The bust of Shakespeare has no permanent resting place, but for many years it has resided beside the walk leading to the large log building across the drive from the McPherson statue.

Brice attempted to carve Shakespeare from an old tombstone. He soon discovered that marble was extremely hard to carve compared to the Black Hand Sandstone he was used to. It quickly dulled his tools and frustrated the sculptor to the point of giving up before finishing. The bust is recognizable as Shakespeare even though unfinished.

It's not known how Brice got the marble tombstone, but some of the inscription is still readable and appears to say: "…May 16, 183?…in the 34th year of her age."

CANNON MOUNTS

Brice constructed two cannon mounts in the park. One is located along the edge of the hill near the statue of Grant. Its inscription reads: "PRESENTED BY W. C. MOONEY, M. C. 1916." This pedestal once held a 1300-pound Civil War era cannon from Waterfelt, New York. Displayed alongside the cannon was a large artillery shell from WWI.

The second cannon mount is located at the west end of the amphitheater and has been fitted more recently with a water faucet. The inscription

Above: Unfinished marble bust of William Shakespeare made from an old tombstone.
(Nathan Keirns photo '98)

Opposite: Close-up of Shakespeare showing tombstone inscription.
(A. Keirns photo '97)

Above: East cannon mount.
(A. Keirns photo '01)

Top Right: East cannon mount as it looked originally. Notice WWI artillery shell beside cannon.

Below: West cannon mount. Notice water faucet just to the right of center near bottom of top block.
(A. Keirns photo '01)

on this pedestal reads: "COL. H. L. EVANS 1924." Colonel Evans was once in charge of the Barracks at Columbus, Ohio. The cannon that rested on this pedestal weighed 700 pounds and came from Fort Harrison.

During World War II, metal for manufacturing weapons and equipment was desperately needed. Scrap metal drives were held across the country. Brice donated both canons to the scrap drive.

WATERING TROUGH

Hidden in the weeds across the driveway from the Lincoln monument lies a large, hollowed out, rectangular-shaped rock. Brice carved this ingenious trough to hold water for the farm animals. The trough is fed by a spring and still contains water today.

STONE VASES

According to former owners of Baughman Park, Brice carved several stone flower vases. These vases were located in various places around the park but were carried off by people during the years when the park was abandoned. We presently have no pictures of these vases.

INSCRIBED WALL

The amphitheater in the area of the Grant statue was often used for group gatherings. A set of steps leads up to an area where a low sandstone wall is inscribed with the following statement: "MEMORIAL PARK, NAMED BY CHAS. LONG, NEWARK, O."

GHOST ROCK

Last, and certainly least, a few words need to be said about the odd-looking rock sitting on the hillside near the entrance to the park. After entering the park from State Route 586, and traveling a short distance along the drive, some visitors have noticed a strange rock peering down at them from the hill on the left side of the drive. This rock is most visible during the colder months when the foliage is down.

At first glance, this rock looks like a pointy-headed ghost with hollow eyes and gaping mouth. From a distance it looks like it might be one of Brice's carvings – but it isn't. The Ghost Rock is an odd but natural formation, carved by the hand of nature to spook us humans.

Above: Stone watering trough.
(A. Keirns photo '98)

Top Left: Inscribed wall.
(Nathan Keirns photo '98)

Bottom Left: Ghost Rock.
(A. Keirns photo '00)

Baughman Memorial Park
Muskingum County, Ohio

- Ghost Rock
- Quarry
- Harding
- Roosevelt
- Lincoln
- McKinley
- Misc. Carvings
- Republican Corner
- Stone Trough
- Old Funeral Home
- State Route 586
- Main Driveway
- Quarry Drive
- Not to Scale
- © 2001 Little River Publishing

76

Sherman

The Doughboy

Washington

Grant

Inscribed Wall

Noah's House

Cat

McPherson

Cannon Mount

Garfield

Brice's House

Well House

Lion

Main Driveway

Shakespeare

Modern Log Cabin

Unfinished Log Building

Old Log Shed

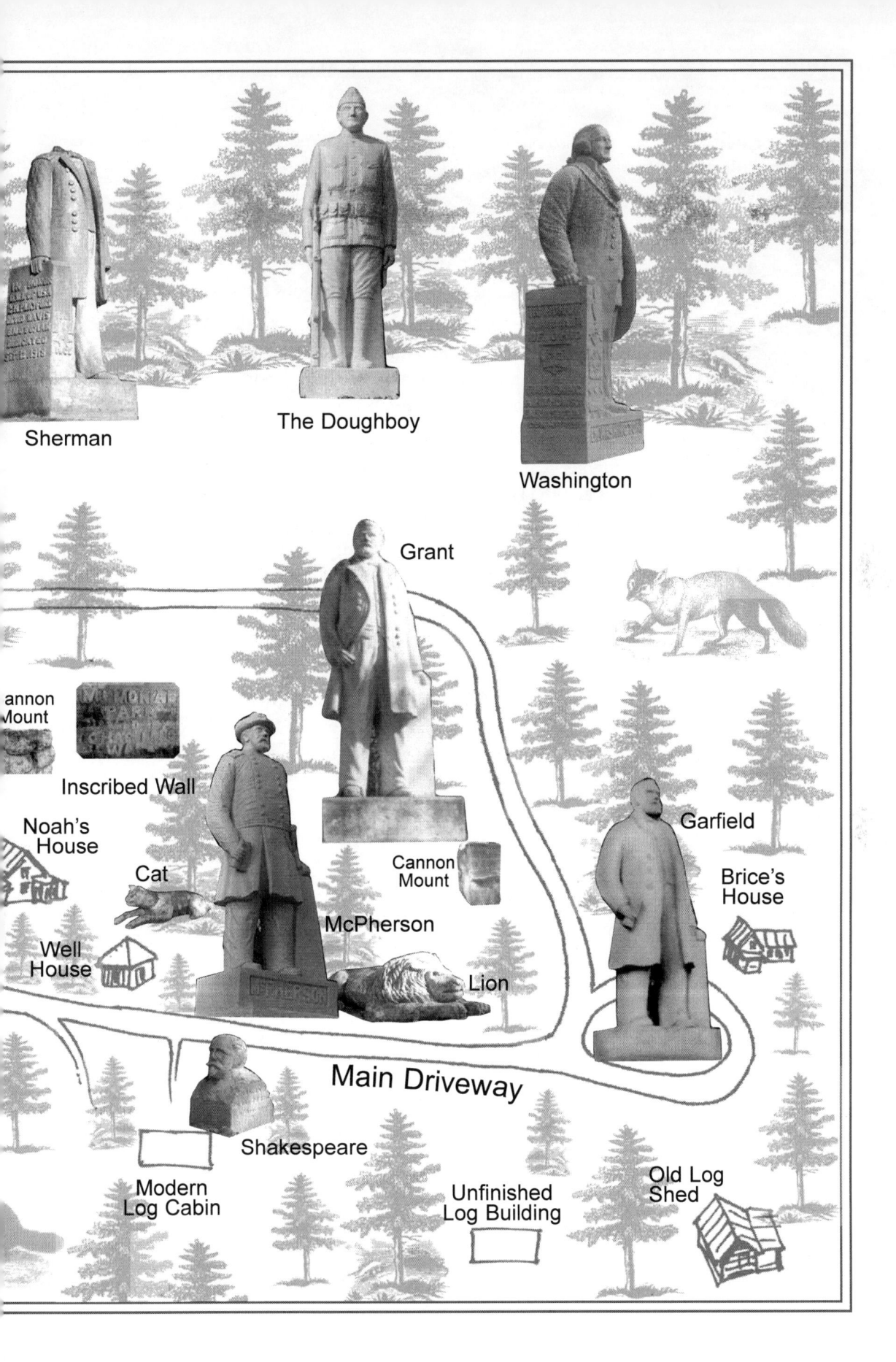

77

ABOUT THE AUTHOR

Aaron Keirns is a native Ohioan with a life-long interest in the history of the Buckeye State.

He is also the author of other popular books, including:

"Black Hand Gorge...A Journey Through Time" and "Ohio's Airship Disaster."

Aaron holds a degree in Anthropology and is a writer, publisher, graphic designer and entertaining speaker.

He and his wife, Bernice, have four children: Adam, Tracy, Jesse and Nathan – and four grandchildren: Elisa, Siaira, Ethan and Aiden.

Speaking Engagements

The author is available for speaking engagements. For more information, visit our web site at:
www.littleriverpublishing.com

ACKNOWLEDGMENTS

There were many people who helped make this book a reality. My sincerest appreciation goes out to all of you.

First and foremost I would like to thank Lester Baughman for sharing his knowledge and time with me. Lester welcomed me into his home, time after time, and patiently answered my many questions. Without his help and encouragement, this book would not exist.

I would also like to thank Bill Weaver and Anita Rector of The Longaberger Company. They generously allowed me access to their archives and the Baughman Park property. Over the years, Bill and I have explored the nooks and crannies of Licking and Muskingum Counties in the heat, rain, mud and snow. This has not been our first adventure together, and hopefully it will not be our last.

Ray and Gloria Murray were also a tremendous help. Ray's collection of photographs and personal insights into the history of the park have added immeasurably to the book.

My old friends, Chance Brockway and Curtis "Bud" Abbott, provided some of the photographs used in the book. These two gents helped me many times over the years and I feel fortunate that I got to know them before they passed on.

Richard and Sararose Hewitt, my good friends from Toboso, steered me in the right direction when I first began looking for Baughman Park. My sons, Jesse and Nathan accompanied me to the park and helped take pictures and gather information. My wife, Bernice, assisted me with some of the research and even spent a snowy day copying the inscriptions from every statue.

The folks at the reference desk at the main library in Zanesville were particularly helpful, as was the staff of the genealogical library. Thanks also to the Newark Library, the Library of Mt. Vernon and Knox County, and the Ohio Historical Center.

As always, a sincere thanks to my family for allowing me the time to pursue these book-writing adventures!

ACKNOWLEDGMENTS

LESTER E. BAUGHMAN
1915-2003

❖

Lester Baughman is shown here, standing on the front porch of his childhood home during a walk with the author through Baughman Park.

When Lester was a boy, he and his brother, Harold, had a little stand at the park where they sold ice cream to visitors. "One summer we made ten dollars!" Lester recalls proudly.

These kinds of historical anecdotes can't be found in old books, newspapers or public records. They only exist in the memories of those who were there. It's simple memories like these that add color to the sepia tone of history. Thanks, Lester, for sharing your colorful memories with us.

Glossary of Terms

anachronism - A person or thing that is chronologically out of place.

bas-relief - Sculptural relief in which the projection is slight, with no undercutting.

Black Hand Gorge - A gorge in Licking County, Ohio, from which Black Hand Conglomerate takes its name.

block and tackle - Pulley blocks with associated ropes or cables.

B. P. O. E. - Benevolent and Protective Order of Elks, a fraternal organization.

conglomerate - A rock composed of rounded fragments of various sizes.

derrick - A hoisting apparatus employing a tackle (pulleys & ropes) rigged at the end of a beam.

doughboy - Slang term used in reference to infantrymen, especially during World War 1.

Elks - Fraternal organization (see B. P. O. E.).

embalm - To treat (a dead body) so as to protect from decay.

F. and A. M. - Free and Accepted Masons, a fraternal organization.

foreshortening - Visual contraction of an object viewed as extended in a plane nearly parallel to the line of sight.

Freemason - Member of the Free and Accepted Masons, a fraternal organization.

funeral parlor - An establishment with facilities for the preparation of the dead (funeral home).

G. A. R. - Grand Army of the Republic, an organization of veterans of America's Civil War.

glacier - A large body of ice moving slowly down a slope or valley or spreading outward on a land surface.

G. O. P. - Grand Old Party, a reference to the Republican Party.

inscription - The wording (as on a statue).

in-the-round - A full sculptured form, unattached to a background.

marble - Limestone that is crystallized and capable of taking a high polish.

Mason - A member of the Free and Accepted Masons, a fraternal organization.

Masonic - Relating to, or characteristic of, Freemasons or Freemasonry.

mallet - A wooden hammer with a large round head.

medium - Any material used for artistic expression.

outcrop - The part of a rock formation that appears at the surface of the ground.

porous - Permeable to fluids, capable of being penetrated.

quarry - An open excavation for obtaining stone.

quarrying - The business, occupation or act of extracting material from a quarry.

raconteur - A person who excels in telling anecdotes.

sandstone - A sedimentary rock consisting of quartz sand united by silica or calcium carbonate.

sedimentary - Formed by deposits of sediment.

Spanish-American War - The war between the United States and Spain, 1898.

stonemason - A mason who builds with stone.

suffrage - The right of voting or the exercise of such right.

suffragist - One who advocates extension of suffrage, especially to women.

undertaker - One whose business is to prepare the dead for burial and manage funerals (funeral director).

WWI - World War One. The war between the Allies (Great Britain, France, Russia, the U. S., Italy, etc.) and the Central Powers (Germany, Austria-Hungary, etc.) 1914-1918.

WWII - World War Two. The war between the Allies (Great Britain, France, the Soviet Union, the U. S., etc.) and the Axis (Germany, Japan, Italy, etc.) 1939-1945.

BIBLIOGRAPHY

Books:

CAMPEN, RICHARD N., "Outdoor Sculpture in Ohio,"
West Summit Press, Chagrin Falls, Ohio, 1980.

CONNER, E. W. "Souvenir Program, Baughman's Memorial Park,"
Frazeysburg, Ohio, 1931.

CONNER, E. W. "Souvenir Program, Frazeysburg Homecoming,"
Frazeysburg, Ohio, 1935.

EVERHART, J. F., "History of Muskingum County, Ohio,"
Unigraphic, Evansville, Indiana, 1974.

FREIDEL, Frank, "The Presidents of the United States of America,"
White House Historical Assn., Washington D. C., 1987.

KEIRNS, Aaron J., "Black Hand Gorge – A Journey Through Time,"
Little River Publishing, Howard, Ohio, 1999.

LEWIS, Thomas W., "History of Southeastern Ohio and the Muskingum Valley,"
S. J. Clarke Publishing Co., Chicago, 1928

PEACEFULL, Leonard (editor), "A Geography of Ohio,"
The Kent State University Press, Kent, Ohio, 1996.

SCHNEIDER, Norris Franz, "Y Bridge City,"
World Publishing Company, Cleveland, c. 1950.

STOUT, "Geology of Muskingum County,"
Zanesville, Ohio, 1912.

SUTOR, J. Hope "Past and Present of Muskingum County, Ohio,"
Windmill Publications, Mt. Vernon, Indiana, 2000.

WARD, Geoffrey, C., "The Civil War,"
Alfred A. Knopf Publishing, New York, 1990.

Articles:

GOLDSTEIN, Ezra "Presidents in the Woods,"
American Heritage, April, 1996.

GOLDSTEIN, Ezra "An Artist's Monumental Effort,"
Ohio Magazine, March, 1997.

Miscellaneous:

JORDAN, Angie and RECTOR, Andrea, "Baughman Memorial Park,"
The Longaberger Company, Newark, Ohio. (unpublished research)

"Stonemasons of Muskingum County Ohio in the 1800's,"
Muskingum Co. Genealogical Chapt. of the Ohio Genealogical Society,
Zanesville, Ohio, 1997

Made in the USA